WITHDRAWN
UTSA LIBRARIES

LOBENGULA.

AMONG THE MATABELE

BY THE
REV. D. CARNEGIE
For Ten Years Resident at Hope Fountain
Twelve Miles from Bulawayo

WITH PORTRAITS OF LOBENGULA AND KHAMA

AND

MAP AND ILLUSTRATIONS

NEGRO UNIVERSITIES PRESS
WESTPORT, CONNECTICUT

Originally published in 1894
by The Religious Tract Society, London

Reprinted in 1970 by
Negro Universities Press
A Division of Greenwood Press, Inc.
Westport, Connecticut

Library of Congress Catalogue Card Number 74-97399

SBN 8371-5094-9

Printed in the United States of America

EDITOR'S PREFACE.

THE Rev. D. Carnegie, the author of this book, went out to Hope Fountain, Matabeleland, in 1882, and spent the next ten years at that station of the London Missionary Society. He has just returned after his first furlough. Hope Fountain is only twelve miles from Bulawayo, the great kraal of Lobengula. Mr. Carnegie knows the native language perfectly, and has been in constant friendly relations with Lobengula, who, although he will have nothing to do with Christianity, is quite sagacious enough to see that the missionary can be of service to him in many ways. Probably no other European knows so well as Mr. Carnegie the Matabele customs, modes of thought, and way of life. The chapters in this little book are all the result of first-hand and thoroughly competent knowledge; they will enable the reader to form accurate ideas about the Matabele people.

The greater portion of the book has appeared in the pages of *The Leisure Hour* and *The Sunday at Home*, and Chapter IX., sketching the life and work of Khama, which is added for the sake of completeness, is from the pen of the Rev. G. Cousins.

CONTENTS.

CHAPTER I.
THE RISE OF THE MATABELE TRIBE 13

CHAPTER II.
ÑI TUSA BABA 21

CHAPTER III.
WITCHCRAFT AND RAIN-MAKING 31

CHAPTER IV.
ARTS AND CRAFTS 53

CHAPTER V.
THE WAR DANCE AND THE FIRST FRUITS . . 70

CHAPTER VI.
MATABELE WOMEN AND CHILDREN . . . 80

CHAPTER VII.

SICKNESS AND DEATH 90

CHAPTER VIII.

CHRISTIAN WORK AMONG THE MATABELE . . . 99

CHAPTER IX.

KHAMA, THE BECHWANA CHRISTIAN CHIEF . . 111

LIST OF ILLUSTRATIONS.

Lobengula	*Frontispiece*
Map of South Africa	*page* 10, 11
A Matabele Village	,, 30
A Matabele Rain Doctor	,, 37
A Group of Matabele and other Warriors . .	,, 52
A Matabele Blacksmith	,, 56
Matabele Weapons	,, 59
A Matabele Youth	,, 87
Mr. Carnegie's Waggon *en route* for Matabeleland	,, 98
Khama	,, 110

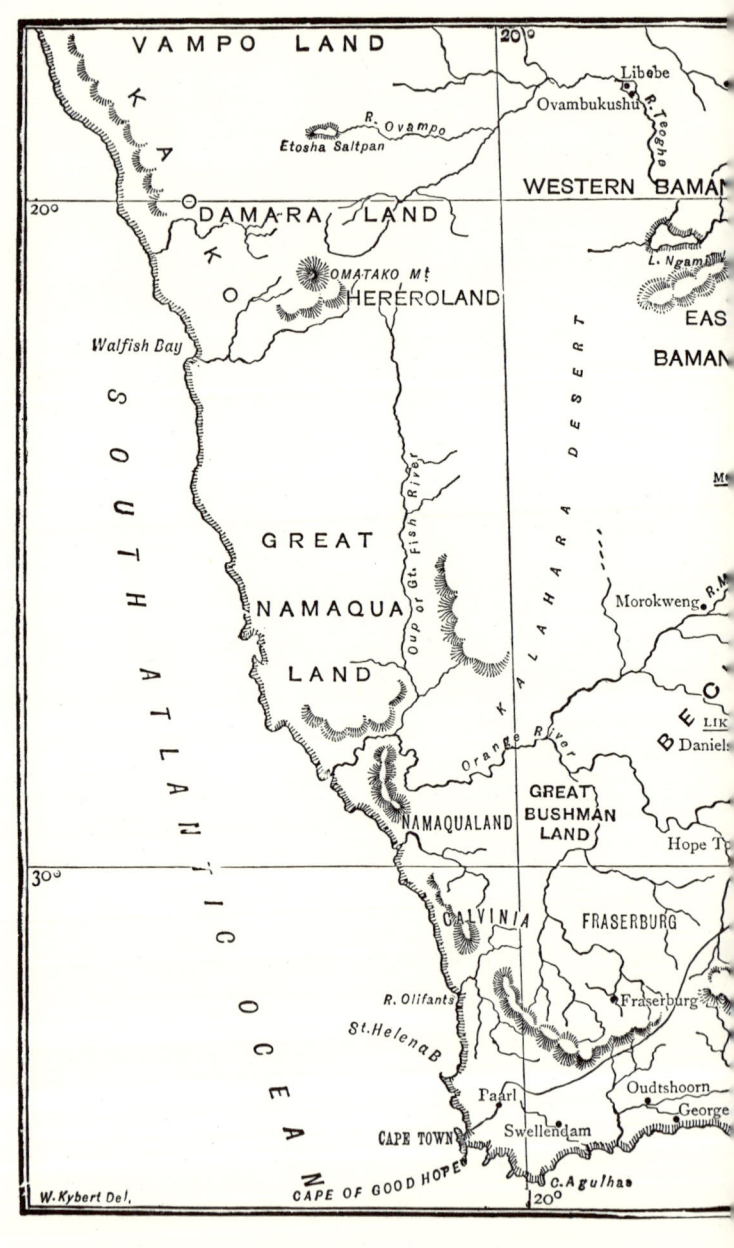

AMONG THE MATABELE.

CHAPTER I.

THE RISE OF THE MATABELE TRIBE.

DURING the first decade of the present century what is now known as Natal and Zululand was inhabited by several small tribes, each having its own induna, or petty chief, between which for many years peace and prosperity reigned. Amongst the tribe that lived at the foot of the Lentemba mountains was a man whose military prowess was destined to revolutionise the face of the whole of these two countries. Tchaka, or Chaka, was his name. He laid waste most of the territory of Natal, crossed the Tugela river, and established the Zulu kingdom.

Under Chaka, belonging to the tribe of Machobana, Umzilikazi (Moselekatse), the father of the present Matabele king, served as an induna, and had command of one of his trusted regiments. Umzilikazi was a shrewd commander, and soon won high military honour in connection with Chaka's mode of heathen warfare, which consisted chiefly in capturing slaves, mostly women and children, and plundering cattle, sheep, and goats.

Somewhere about the year 1825, Chaka sent out this great general with a large 'impi' towards the north on another raiding expedition, which proved a great success, large herds of cattle, flocks of sheep, and many captives being stolen. This took place some days' journey from the great kraal of Chaka. It was the custom of the tribe that all booty belonging to his impis should be handed over to the chief; but now Umzilikazi, flushed with success and feeling almost every inch a king himself, determined upon another plan, and sent only one half of all this captured booty, while he waited on the outskirts of the country with his army for the result. A great battle ensued, hundreds were slain on both sides; and feeling he was now a rival with Chaka for the Zulu throne, and that if he did return and give himself up it would mean death, Umzilikazi turned his back upon the land of his fathers for ever, and started on his long and chequered march northwards. Crossing the Drachensberg mountains, he fought his way up through what is now known as the Orange Free State and Transvaal; and for some years he settled down in the district of Marico, near Zeerust, in the northern part of the Transvaal. While here he continued his raiding on the tribes around, by means of which his scattered forces were strengthened, and his flocks and herds increased. His army grew in numbers and prospered.

About the year 1837 a large company of Boers left Cape Colony to seek a new and a better country, and ultimately arrived not far from the vicinity of Umzilikazi, where they intended to form a new republic,

THE RISE OF THE MATABELE TRIBE. 15

which is now the Transvaal. These new-comers proved a thorn in the side of Umzilikazi; and after a pitched battle, in which he was completely routed, he left Marico, crossed the Crocodile, and continued his march northwards, until he arrived in the country where he established what is now known as the Matabele nation.

Establishing himself in his new quarters meant driving out the Amaswazi, whom he found inhabiting the land, but who afterwards returned, begged for mercy, and became incorporated into the nation, like many other petty tribes which he subdued in his immediate neighbourhood. Gradually he built up his military system, forming new regiments, and quelling insurrections. He forbade his young warriors to marry, and governed his people with a rod of iron. His activity was everywhere felt. Often he would arrive at some out-of-the-way village quite unexpectedly in the early morning, to see the people and look at the cattle. His name soon struck fear into the peace-loving tribes of the Banyai, Makalaka, and Magoma or Mashona, most of whom are now but scattered remnants of peoples living in different parts of the country. There were at least nine or ten different chiefs conquered by the mighty spear of this powerful monarch, some of whom represented tribes of ten, fifteen, or twenty thousand people, most of whom lived on the east, north, and north-east of Hhahlandlela, which was then the capital of the country.

From this chief's advent into the country about the year 1837 little or nothing is known till Dr. Moffat's first visit in 1854. Like Chaka, Umzilikazi was a cruel, despotic man, with low views of human life and justice, whose practice it was to exterminate women and men, and bring up their children in the ranks of his soldiers. It is said of him when well advanced in years, some time after the missionaries had settled in the country, that on one occasion he was visibly affected by the innocent play of one of their children, and that just then some of his own men came to report a certain matter, on which he gave orders to execute a person charged with some minor offence, because it suited his whim. Some months before his death, while speaking with one of the missionaries, he pointed out to him a young lad who was then herding the goats and sheep, and added, 'Mnali, do you see that boy there?' 'Yes,' was the reply, 'I see him.' 'Do you know who he is?' 'No, I do not know him.' 'I will tell you,' the chief went on. 'That is my own son, Lobengula, who, when I am gone, is to rule this kingdom.' Having said that he sat and looked with earnest eyes for a long time on Lobengula, who was to rule in his stead for the next twenty years.

When the present chief, Lobengula, succeeded to the throne of his father, he became the absolute monarch of all he surveyed, and to dispute his right to anything and everything, for anybody and everybody, meant either banishment or death. His first step on ascending the throne was to quell the insurrection of a party who believed the real heir to be Kuruman, an elder brother who was absent during Lobengula's coronation. Umbigo, as brave a soldier as ever stepped, led the opposition; his followers were

THE RISE OF THE MATABELE TRIBE.

like him, and they fought for Kuruman to the bitter end. The chief sent out two large armies in opposite directions, which were to meet on each side of Zwanandaba, Umbigo's town, which was situated some fifteen miles from Bulawayo, and contained the most courageous regiment of Matabele warriors then living in the country. It is needless to add that after a hard deadly hand-to-hand struggle, in which hundreds of brave men fell, including Umbigo himself, Lobengula was victorious. This action on his part struck terror into all the indunas and headmen of the tribe, and through them into the common people who trembled with fear. During the years that followed Lobengula weeded out—knocked on the head—many old men who did yeoman service in the battles his father fought. This is not all, he caused his own sister to be killed, and eight or nine of his brothers suffered death at his hands. From my own personal observation I know that there was a yearly black list of scores of persons who suffered death for witchcraft. By such means he upheld his heathen monarchy. When some innocent victim had been clubbed to death for witchcraft, the people, if asked the reason, said in substance: 'We don't know, we are but slaves and vassals of the king, we have no voice in the matter, our customs were created with us. Besides, it's the chief's business, he knows. It must be right if he does it, for he is the chief who cannot err.' They feared and dreaded him, they swore by him, in their eyes he had a divine right to act as he pleased; he was their god who ruled by fear, overrode justice, killed the innocent, plundered his peaceful neighbours' cattle; was, in fact, as far as it suited his cunning heathen craftiness, the same sort of a monster as his father had been.

Round this heathen monarch and his counsellors cling tenaciously superstition, witchcraft, and caste, which are other names for what we term the government of the country, which really is no government worthy of the name, but a patched-up combination of heathen laws and customs, of self-conceitedness, pride, and arrogance and ignorance, upheld by fear and terror, guarded by jealousy and revenge, and the frequent sacrifice of human life. Their past success in war, which is mainly owing to their rushing at day-break upon some unsuspecting neighbour while he is scarcely yet awake, has engendered this feeling of pride among the people to an unlimited extent. Their pride is limitless. In speaking of themselves they say, 'The Matabele are great and powerful, their sharp-pointed spear and mighty shield are dreaded by everybody. No one can stand before us in battle. We are warriors; beyond our country live the cowards, the dogs, and the slaves. We are men; those yonder are but slaves and dogs, and must be treated as such. Who is like our great king? You may as well try to stop the onward march of that sun through the heavens as to try and contend against his power. The king, is he not god? has he not power to bring the clouds, and cause the rains to fill the rivers? Is he not our great rain-maker? Do we speak of him merely as the child of the great king Umzilikazi? When we address him do we not say—

Zulu. The heavens.
Hhabezulu. The spearer of the heavens (rain-maker).
Babamkulu. Great father.
Mamamkulu. Great mother.
Inkosinkulu. Great king.
Inkosinkululenyaña. Great black king.
Inkosiyamakosi. King of kings.
Inkosi wezulu yomhlaba. King of heaven and earth.'

There is no end to the titles he possesses; and their flattering phraseology knows no limits, especially when any of his subjects are begging for anything, such as an ox skin to make a shield with, or food— Kaffir corn—on account of hunger, or native picks to dig their gardens.

The most critical event during Lobengula's reign prior to the war in 1893, took place in the latter end of 1890, when the British South African pioneers passed along the eastern border of his country to Mashonaland. Whether or not he consented to their taking that route, one thing is certain, that he succeeded in maintaining peace, that is, in keeping in check his people, who were full of excitement and blood-thirstiness to go to war with the approaching white man; but as often as they begged to be allowed to go on the war-path, as often were they refused permission to go.

Lobengula and his people know much about white men in general, and Englishmen in particular; about their guns and ammunition, their articles of manufacture, beads, clothing, carpentering, and smithing. They know how the Zulu power went down; and we might imagine they would conclude that the day for trusting in spears and shields was fast passing away.

This, however, is not the case; instead the old heathen habits and customs are adhered to, the plough of progress has no place in the land, and the people are very much in the position they occupied twenty years ago. What things they do buy and borrow from civilisation are used, or abused rather, under the heavy yoke of government, against which no one dares to raise his voice. An induna, speaking to me on one occasion about the power of the king, stated that he was afraid to say anything on behalf of others whom he knew were unjustly condemned to die, because of witchcraft, and to be silent meant to save his own head. There are many rich people in the land who have lots of cattle with which to buy waggons, and ploughs, and spades, but they dare not—only the chief may buy waggons; and as for agricultural implements, the people are not allowed to buy them. Such things are below the dignity of his heathen majesty, who with no hesitation accepts the blessings of civilisation, while at the same time he ignores its laws, liberty, and progress.

CHAPTER II.

Ñi TUSA BABA.

ONE of the first words you learn in Sintebele, the language spoken by the Matabele, and which you hear on arriving in the country, is *tusa*, which means 'give me a present.' Their reason for having this begging propensity so largely developed is, 'Because,' they say, 'we white people were created in the long ago—long before them, which accounts for us having so many good things, and they so few.' They ask you for everything, from a needle to an ox; and those who are most generous in their *tusas* are besieged the most by crowds of people, from sun-up to sun-down, for calico, beads, waistcoats, hats, knives, tobacco, snuff, beer (made from Kaffir corn); in fact, everything they see you have which they have not they beg for. From the queens and head indunas down to the meanest slave, men and women, and boys and girls, all of them are persistent beggars, and the more you give them the worse they are.

Visiting and begging are two important functions among them. A man will come to your place, sit down outside your door, and shout out, *O guble Baba*, meaning thereby, 'I hope it is well with you.' When they visit you, you are supposed to be the first to speak. You say, *Sagubona*, literally, 'I see you;' to more than one, *Sagubonani*, 'I see you all.' When you go to see the chief or among the towns, you are greeted first by them. After being some days from home, on your return they greet you first. When your guests leave, you bid them *Hambani guhle*, 'Go ye nicely,' and they reply, *Salani guhle*, 'Stay ye nicely.' There are other expressions used, such as

> *U se kona na?* Are you there?
> *U sezwa na?* Are you hearing?
> *U sa hamba guhle na?* Are you going well?
> *U sa hamba emzimbeni na?* How are you in your body?

This formal greeting over, the next question is, 'What are you eating? when had you beef in your town? or when had you beer?' The reply to this is, 'Oh, we have nothing; it's hunger with us; we are being killed by it!' If you have just returned from visiting the chief, you may say, 'I have been eating beef and drinking beer.' When visiting the chief, he puts before you as a rule a wooden dish full of roast beef, and you are expected to help yourself with fingers and pocket-knife.

You are supposed also, as a matter of etiquette, to drink beer out of a calabash which is put before you. This beer is an important thing in the land. It is looked upon as an article of food, and is in common use among the natives, who are very fond of it. To despise it means despising food; it is amongst the things they beg for when coming to pay you a visit. They may visit you, in fact, for the express purpose of getting a good drink of it, and if you do not buy it you will be spared many a begging call, which may mean much when you have more serious business to attend to than their oft-repeated requests for *tusas*.

Once I was travelling with a man when he picked up a certain grass and stuck it in his woolly hair. On asking what he meant by this, he informed me that before sunset he would be sure to drink beer. This was the sign for it. At another time when I was nearing the end of a twelve-mile walk, my stick fell out of my hand on to the ground. My boy who was with me at once remarked, 'We shall feast this evening on good things.' Soon it fell out a second time, when he added, 'Without a doubt we shall eat lots this evening.'

They beg from one another also. Beef and beer as articles of food are things in common among them. Parties on passing a town where there is beer-drinking going on will call there, and as a matter of custom join the merry company. I have often asked passers-by where they were going. Oh, they were going to such and such a village. Why? Because they heard they had slaughtered oxen and were eating beef. Their usual way of begging for food is by patting their bare stomachs with their flat hand, and bending themselves inwards, to demonstrate in a practical way that they are empty and hungry. 'There is a cold in my stomach, do give me some food to warm it; I am killed by hunger; I have travelled far, and am very tired.'

If a person arrives late in the evening, you are bound by the law of the land to give him sleeping quarters for the night; or if he has lost his way, you may not refuse him food and shelter.

More than once have they begged soap, sugar, and English vegetables out of my garden. Lobengula enjoys cabbages, and drinks coffee, and has often had a loaf of bread from my wife, which he relishes very much. But in regard to vegetables, some of the natives are beginning to like them too well, for they were not contented with getting some at a plentiful time, but they stole from our garden when they could.

Famine, though much talked about, is very seldom seen in the country. And for this reason; if the crops in one district fail they are good in another, and those who have no corn ask the chief for oxen, with which they buy from those who have. When there is a good general harvest all over the land, it is accompanied with much drunkenness and many quarrels, since the traders sometimes use brandy indiscriminately in trading with the natives.

Sometimes they try flattery, in hope of getting a *tusa*. Here is an instance. A man whose brother was being doctored by the missionary called to see how he was getting along. Before leaving, he went and said good-bye in this style to the missionary: 'Teacher, you are a nice man, your medicine has saved my brother's life; you are of us, you belong to us, you are the king's teacher, you are generous and kind. Long ago I heard of the fame of your medicines. You see,' he continued, 'I have come to say good-bye to you. I could never think of leaving your place without doing that; my heart is white towards you. Now you know, teacher, I know you will be sorry to hear I lost my knife the other day, and I ask you, as a great favour, to *tusa* me with another one.' If they succeed in their begging, they laugh behind your back, and say that you are a fool.

The soil is very well suited for all kinds of European seeds; you need never be without green vegetables all the year round; fruit-trees grow luxuriantly, grapes and oranges and bananas flourish abundantly. The land is rich, with deep soil, the valleys are well-watered, and fountains bubble up everywhere. Irrigation can be made easy; hundreds and thousands of cattle, sheep, and bucks graze around, and many more would, but for the primitive mode of rearing live stock.

The *amabele*, or Kaffir corn, is the staple food. One of the most important things in the eyes of a native is his patch of ground with corn sown in it. Besides this, he sows mealies, Indian corn, beans, melons, pumpkins, sweet reed, and a kind of vegetable marrow. They are careful in preserving their *amabele*, which they store away in the cattle-kraal underground, in holes that in shape resemble a balloon turned upside down. These corn-bins are six feet deep, and about nine in diameter, though some are larger than others; some will contain thirty *muids*, others twelve or fifteen. They are covered down from sight in the enclosure where the cattle sleep by bark and stone, and hermetically sealed. Corn in this condition remains intact for two years; and its peculiar flavour is preferred to that which is stored away in the large potclay-made bins exposed to the sun. In a scarce year they buy corn with oxen, which they kill, cut up and divide out for basketfuls, which they bring for barter.

The garden is a most important piece of land, and if any cattle or buck get in to eat the corn, woe be to the herd-boy, whoever he may be. My trek oxen were once driven into a garden, just for the purpose of making me pay, which I had to do, or else lose some of them. A white man, whose oxen, eight in number, were chased through nine different gardens, some of which belonged to the queens, had to pay a blanket for every one entered. Often herd-boys, rather than face the consequence of allowing their oxen to eat the corn, flee the country; others are maimed for life, while others die from the effects of an unmerciful thrashing. If oxen or sheep enter the gardens during the day, the herd is responsible, but if they break out in the night and find their way into any garden, then the owner of the oxen has to pay for the damage done.

If they thrash your herd-boy, then you have not to pay; if you pay them for the damage, then you save your boy's back. If you have a quarrel with a work-boy, who grumbles at his pay, which he agreed for on his coming to you for work, he may play you a mean trick the night before he leaves, by opening up your kraal-gate, and letting your herd go into a garden.

On one occasion some of my cows got out in the night and found their way into a native garden. The owner of it was a queen, who came next day and knocked at my door, and called me to see her. On opening it, I found her sitting on the ground with any-thing but a pleasant smile on her face. 'Well, how are you to-day?' I inquired. She replied, 'I have not come to visit nor to see you ; I have come for my corn, my food ; your oxen have eaten me up ; all my garden is finished clean off ; I have nothing to eat ; I have come to ask you for my corn.' The fact was my cows had scarcely eaten any of her corn, it was only her native way of talking. *A pelile dò :* 'It is finished every whit.' After some tall talk I gave her a yard and a half of calico, and she went away satisfied.

Lazy persons, who will not help in sowing or reaping are driven from town to town. No work, no food, is the motto for them. The queens themselves dig their gardens ; and everybody who can must help to prepare for the dry season, which begins towards the end of April, and ends about the middle of October.

Potatoes begin to multiply among the towns, they thrive very well, and are much sought after by the white population. The chief uses them too. The sweet potatoes also, the white and red kind, both grow, and one likes them once in a way, but tires of them after a while.

It is wonderful how the native beer seems to fatten them. To be córpulent in their eyes is to be graceful, and some of the old wives of the chiefs, to my knowledge, weigh over 250 lbs. You may imagine then what their idea of a graceful figure is, for the custom in dress is to go with the upper part of the body entirely bare, while round the waist and loins they tie a few yards of white or spotted calico, and one or two dirty tiger-cat or other skins.

The land, if properly cultivated, would yield

splendid harvests of wheat, oats and barley. Sow wheat in May, reap it in November; plough again, and reap another harvest in March. You may have two crops a year, and good ones too, provided you attend to your land as you ought to do. Your orchard, moreover, will provide you with all kinds of peaches, also apricots, apples, pears, almonds, quinces, walnuts; besides, you can have mulberries, Cape gooseberries, and other fruits. I am speaking now of Bulawayo and the watershed into Fort Salisbury, in Mashonaland. No doubt coffee, tea, and cocoa would also grow if they were planted; and the settler may reckon on fir, spruce, larch, and other kinds of trees thriving as well.

So far as the production of foods is concerned, the natives only scratch with their hand-picks a wee bit on the surface, while most of the fertile valleys lie waste for want of tillage.

A MATABELE VILLAGE.

CHAPTER III.

WITCHCRAFT AND RAIN-MAKING.

THE Matabele belief in witchcraft is marvellous. To tell a man he is a thief, a rogue, a liar, has a wicked heart, means very little, and impresses him far less than to call him a witch. What is a witch? He is a person who roams about at night, is in league with a wolf, who is in communication with the spirits of the departed, who goes to their graves to ask power to bewitch others, who possesses certain medicines, with powerful bewitching properties. Such an one they firmly believe has power to bewitch people, so that they die as a consequence; and cattle, sheep, goats, gardens, all these may suffer from the blighting influence of the witch. A man who is suspected of witchcraft has a very miserable existence, and at any time may be driven away from his town, out of the country, or thrown to the wolves—for witches they do not bury.

They believe certain medicines have the power to bewitch. Sprinkling the blood of an ox in the yard, outside or inside their huts, in the cattle enclosure, or among the sheep, is rank witchcraft, deserving of death. As I was sitting one day with the chief, a man arrived, and reported the following case: 'Oh! great father, we are in sore trouble at home; certain signs have appeared lately which cause great anxiety in our town. While we were sitting in the induna's hut, all of a sudden blood began dropping from the roof on to the floor, then it trickled and came faster and faster, until it poured down in a great stream, at which we were all afraid, and left the hut.' Such was the report, the result of which was the death of some poor innocent victim, against whom the induna and some others had a grudge.

Here is another case which came under my own observation. An induna's son, when visiting his friends who lived on the outskirts of the country, took by force a spear from one of the slaves there. On returning home he fell ill and died. His people attributed his death to the taking (stealing) of that spear, the owner of which bewitched him, so that he died. This I heard from the young man's friends themselves, who declared it was witchcraft and nothing else that caused his death.

The person who is in league with the wolf is dreaded very much by the people. His method of bewitching is this: after dark, when everybody is supposed to turn into their huts, he steals quietly out, follows up the wolf in the footpath, mounts it, drives it round the town; and just outside, opposite the dwellings of those whom he wants to bewitch, he puts down, or hides in the fence, certain powerful medicines. Then, after accompanying his wolf a short distance on its way back, he returns to his home.

Here is a true incident which happened not a mile away from my own place. One of my young dogs died. In the presence of one of the head men of our neighbouring villages it was cut open and some strychnine sprinkled in it. I called a native, who put it behind my kraal on the top of the hill. In the night a wolf came, ate and died. Only in its hurry to get down to the river it passed through the garden of one of the queens, and died there. The corn was high, and in the morning a hue and cry arose when the queen's girls came to weed her garden. Who sent that wolf there to bewitch her corn? Where did it come from? Whoever dared to send a wolf, the most hideous witch in creation, to die in her garden? There was quite an uproar. They sent for me, and after sundry explanations the matter was settled. The man who was witness to my putting in the poison the evening before came to see it. He gave those who had assembled to see the dead witch an account of my cutting up the dog, and taking so much medicine between my fingers as a pinch of snuff, and all the rest of it, at which they were mightily astonished, and, seeing the fate of the wolf, believed in the wonderful power of the white man's medicines.

While standing looking at the dead wolf there in the long grass—for it was the middle of summer—this same neighbour drew my attention to a mark or a scar in its ear. 'There,' he said, pointing to it, 'is a mark belonging to some one to whom this wolf belongs, and who rides on its back in the night, for the purpose of bewitching.' 'No,' I replied, 'that is only a scratch, received in fighting with other wolves over a bone.' 'No, no, not a bit of it; that mark was put there by some ill-disposed person to distinguish it in the dark from others, so that he might not jump on the wrong one.' It was no use arguing with him, for he believed that the scratch on the wolf's ear was put there by some one; but he was glad nevertheless that I had succeeded in poisoning what they believed to be one of the greatest witches alive.

In this horrible business many an innocent man and woman lose their life. Revenge, jealousy, hatred and covetousness lurk behind this belief in witchcraft, and turn it to deadly uses. No one trusts another, each one is afraid of the other; and the golden rule of love thy neighbour as thyself is quite unknown in the land. Every one carries about with him a stout stick, a knobkerry or spear. They are close-fisted, suspicious, and ever on the watch to kill something or somebody. There is no beauty in birds or beasts, in clouds or flowers, bountiful Nature has no attractions for them; the lovely sunsets, the bright twinkling stars, the leafy trees, and waving grass raise no response in their dull dark breasts.

But let us return to our witchcraft, and trace the process of the different stages of the mock trial through which it passes. They are briefly as follows. Certain men, say ten in number, have a grudge against some one belonging to their town, who may or may not be well connected, but most likely is rich in cattle and sheep, or at least more wealthy, from a native point of view, than any of his accusers. They talk together about him, lay their plans, tip the witch-doctor and set about killing him. They go to the chief, and lay their case before him somewhat after this fashion: 'We are troubled with much sickness, people are dying, cattle are dying, owls are flying about, snakes are appearing, we are bewitched by some one.' The chief may ask by whom, when they give the man's name (the poor innocent man who knows nothing at all about the business), after which the chief refers them to the great smeller-out, the witch-doctor of the country. On arriving at his hut this great doctor, who already has been presented with an ox, knows very well whom to select as the victim. He goes through certain performances, and after much noise and nonsense picks out this poor man, who is absolutely ignorant of the crafty wicked plot of his neighbours and friends. The victim protests against the decision of the witch-doctor, declares his innocence in front of them all, but the wily witch-man, when he sees all the others are with him, upholds his verdict. The unhappy man thus accused returns as a criminal to the chief, and swears by Umzilikazi and everybody else that he knows nothing whatever about these charges; but now all are opposed to him, he pleads alone in front of the king, for whose final decision they wait. It may be, 'Cast him to the wolves' there and then, or a command to kill him at his own town; or he may be pardoned, or he may flee the country; but after such a trial as this his position is lost, the black brand of the witch is upon him, and his life is in jeopardy every day. The most common result is that he is killed, and one or two of his wives with him; his few oxen and sheep are taken by his false accusers, and his home becomes a heap of ruins.

During 1890 thirty such cases came under my personal observation in one month. Under such circumstances, who sees the mothers' tears and hears the wailing cries and sobs of the infants? This is but a meagre sketch of the unjust, cruel, murdering power of witchcraft, which is one of the blackest facts in Matabele heathenism.

There is much superstition in the mind of a Matabele connected with rain-making. Many and varied are the performances transacted in order to bring the clouds and cause the rain. The rainy season, as a rule, begins about the middle of October and ends in April. If no rain falls before November the people begin to grumble, and try to find out some reason for this long delay. The great rain-maker, of course, is the king himself, to him they look for rain; and though it be late in coming, they say it is not because his medicines cannot bring the clouds, he has no power to make it rain, something else is wrong. Some witch is at work upsetting the laws of Nature, whose medicines have a particular charm over the clouds, which prevent them from opening and letting out the rain. Certain obstacles are removed by the people themselves, such as stones and sticks on branches of trees. Crowds of men and boys go round the veldt with knobkerries for the express purpose of knocking down the witches on the ground. Should this fail, they hit on something else. Once a solemn deputation of old women waited on me to warn me against shooting, for they declared that the sound of my gun drove away the clouds. You might as well try and convince a brick wall that the report of my

A MATABELE RAIN-DOCTOR.

gun had nothing whatever to do with the rain falling as convince them, and for peace' sake my innocent gun was put in the rack for some months. They once declared also that the sound of the church bell belonging to the missionaries prevented the clouds from bringing rain. To go to draw water in the river with just a little in the bottom of the calabash keeps away the rain.

There are rain-doctors living in every quarter of the land, who are particularly busy at this season of the year. If the rains are local, which very often is the case, then those doctors in whose districts it has rained have more powerful medicines than those in whose districts it has not rained ; and because of this they receive oxen, while the other doctors get none. But if the rains are plentiful and general all over the country, no rain-doctor is in particular paid or praised. In such a case the chief alone receives all the credit for being so generous in giving all the people an abundant harvest. When it rains they say, 'The king's heart is white, he rejoices, and remembers us, and he is giving us the rain, for which we thank him.'

Here is an interesting incident which happened at the chief's old town at Bulawayo, bearing on this subject of rain-making. A white man was repairing the roof of the chief's house. The rainy season was close at hand. Several powerful rain-doctors (makers) were busy cooking their rain medicine in the yard. This the white men call 'hellbroth.' In swinging round a long pole to put on the roof, this poor carpenter, to the great horror and dismay of these doctors, knocked over this precious pot and spilt all the medicine on the ground. These rain-makers would have felled him to the earth with their kerries, but, though they yelled as only savages can, they dared not strike him in the presence of the chief, who had been watching the proceedings, and seemed to enjoy the joke immensely. Soon after mid-day a tremendous downpour commenced, which continued till nearly sunset, which shower the carpenter afterwards declared would not have fallen if his pole had not upset the rain-makers' medicine pot!

If the chief studies anything, it is the weather. If rain threatens, he collects various kinds of roots, snake-bones, feathers of different birds, the liver of the crocodile, leaves, and the bark of several trees. All this he boils up in a pot, or it may be it is piled up in a heap and burned on the ground. The ingredients of this strange concoction are supposed to have power over the clouds and cause the rain. Should plenty of rain have fallen, however, then it is not necessary to go through this collection of the roots and the rest, or the offering of oblations. If rain has fallen in every district except at headquarters, then the chief calls several rain-doctors whose medicines are supposed never to fail in bringing rain. They ask the chief for an ox of a certain colour or peculiar-shaped horns, or a buck, or a sheep, perhaps a cow, which they slaughter, and in whose blood they mix their medicines; or they may only take a foreleg, or the heart, or the liver, the tail, or some other part of the dead animal; and while this is being cooked they shout and yell, sing a sort of 'hum-drum' song, stamp the ground, and gesticulate. After this

WITCHCRAFT AND RAIN-MAKING.   41

performance if it rains the chief professes to believe in them ; if it does not, then something or somebody is to blame for bewitching their medicines.

In 1883, the white people who were hunting had shot a great many hippopotami, and this the rain-doctors said was the reason why the rains were so long in coming.

As a last resort in making rain, some poor innocent victim is smelt out as a veritable witch and killed. One poor old man, who lived with his young son and some relatives thirty or forty miles from Bulawayo, was cruelly put to death on this account. This person knew nothing whatever of his accusers, who fell upon him, clubbing him to death, burning up his kraal, dividing his property, taking his relatives and odds and ends. All this was done on the false pretext that he had a special kind of plant growing in his garden, the bewitching properties of which were upsetting all the rain-makers' medicines at headquarters.

The people also say if the rainfall is meagre, 'We must have angered our chief, who is punishing us by refusing to send us rain. We have done wrong, for which we must suffer. The chief is angry, his heart is badly disposed,' which to them accounts for the scanty rains of that season. I know that a man once told Umzilikazi not to make more rain, as they had had enough already, and the corn was rotting for lack of sunshine. On receiving this command the old chief said, 'What slave is that who comes to ask me to do this for him? Who is he, and what right has he to dictate to a chief? Go and throw him to the wolves!' And he was killed. A man whom I knew well asked the chief not long ago not to make rain, as he was about to make him some bricks for the purpose of building his waggon house. Many are the secret messengers whom the chief sends away to call certain men belonging to other tribes to come to make rain, and for their roots and rain medicines, which are used at the beginning of the wet season.

Now just in the middle of the rainy season, or we may say between the early and latter rain, at the end of January and in February, the great war dance takes place. This is held at Bulawayo, where people from towns in the land congregate, dressed up in all their finery, which includes black and spotted calico, pink and black beads, twisted round their legs, necks, and arms; skins—monkey, tiger-cat, jenette, buck, sheep—old coats, shirts, hats, and patches of rags of every description. It is the annual gala fair to which they come to thank and praise the chief for sending the rain; they thank him by shouting out his titles; they praise him in songs—war songs principally—and by dancing; but the chief object which many have in view in going there is to drink beer, eat beef, and join in heathen revelry for two or three days. While on their way to this great war dance, they talk about the chief, the rain, their gardens, beer drinking, and oxen they hope to slaughter. If rain overtake them, they are reminded of the generosity of their chief; if they are stopped by a flooded river, they are reminded again that this flowing stream is another display of the mighty power of Lobengula. In fact, on every side they are met with manifestations of his mindfulness of their wants; the young grass is springing up everywhere, the trees are in leaf and blossom; the corn, mealies, and pumpkins are growing fast. Their chief! who is like him, who can spear the heavens like him? He is mighty in battle, no one can equal him in strength and greatness. At the dance they often call him by the titles of Rain, The Full River, Mighty Gushing Sounding Water, The God of Rain, Rain-Maker, and other such high-flown phrases. This war dance is the rivet which clenches in their minds the awful superstition that the chief is really and truly the great rain-maker of the land.

The eyes of a heathen tribe are holden, for they see no beauty or variety in earth or sky. The book of Nature is shut up and sealed; there is no music in the moaning of the wind, rustling among the trees, nor loveliness in the golden-tinted sunsets. Nature's messengers inspire only fear and distrust. The only natural objects they admire are in their gardens at the time when they contain a rich crop of Kaffir corn and mealies, pumpkins and beans. The sun even in his majestic march across the heavens is nothing to them, except in so far as he adds to their health, food, and warmth. Though it is not generally believed, yet many think that by some strange process or other the sun dies every evening, and a new one is born every morning. This opinion, however, is more general in regard to the moon. They believe that the chief creates the new moon every month, and on first seeing it they thank the king, and say they trust the new moon will bring them new beads, blankets, and many presents of nice things from the white people. The cluster of seven stars, the Pleiades—which are called Silimela, *i.e.*, 'Let us dig'—are the signs for them to begin sowing their gardens. Any unnatural appearance, such as an eclipse of the sun or moon, a comet (a star with a tail to it), is looked upon with suspicion. On the strength of Whitaker's Almanack, I once committed myself to them. They denied that there was any truth in the white man's books. 'Look here, you people,' said I, 'let us put it to the test. To-morrow, the book says there will be an eclipse of the sun at midday. If it lies, then never more believe in it; but if not, then be convinced that some of the white man's books do not tell untruths.' To-morrow, at midday, my anxiety was relieved at hearing my herd-boy shouting out, 'What is wrong with the sun? There is a bit out of it, it is broken, and it is setting at midday to-day! All the hens are going to roost, the cattle are coming home, for it is already getting dark.' There was quite a stir about the place. Some were asking, 'What is the matter, what shall we do, where shall we hide?' This was a practical lesson to my sceptical neighbours, who were afterwards more careful in their unguarded statements regarding the wonderful book of the white man.

In the month of March, 1885, a very strange coincidence happened in connection with an eclipse of the moon. The night before full moon—the night before the eclipse—nearly half the nation had been called out on impi, to go towards Lake N'Gami on a raiding expedition, and they were all encamped just on the border of the country. That very evening the eclipse took place. Having set their camp fires ablaze, and made all preparations for sleeping, they sat down on the ground, waiting for the moon to rise. Being long in making her appearance, they began questioning one another thus: 'Where is the moon? Is it not late in coming? Is it not full moon this evening? Where is her light? Why is she not shining on us? What witches are at work? By what means do they prevent her light shining on us?' Such were a few of the questions they were asking each other, when, lo, to the great consternation of every one, there appeared the dim outline of the moon's disc, with the two horns of the eclipse painted red in the far-away eastern sky. This awful phenomenon almost paralysed the whole army. Hundreds of them began grumbling in the following fashion: Some said, 'Oh! my legs tremble; I am no good for the war path; I feel sick; my head aches; I will return home to-morrow.' While others, putting up their hands and clasping them together behind their heads, exclaimed: 'We are bewitched; we shall be defeated in battle; our enemies will overcome us, for their powerful medicines have caused this darkness to blunt our spears, and charm away our strength.' Next day, many actually did turn back, from what proved in the end to be a most disastrous expedition. Hundreds died from thirst during that long march across the Kalahari desert, amongst whom was the king's own brother.

On another occasion an eclipse of the moon took place two months after the impi had left the country on a plundering expedition across the Zambesi.

This, however, was a sign to those at home that the impi had been successful, and that a chief had been slain in battle, which surmise turned out to be true. Before this chief fell under the Matabele spear, he told his would-be murderer that if he killed him he would die on the day that he returned home, which, strange to say, the man did on the very day he arrived at Bulawayo, and just after the native army-doctors had mounted before going into the presence of Lobengula. It is the special work of the army-doctor to sprinkle on the men, by means of a giraffe's tail, some peculiar preparation of roots, by means of which he washes away all their impurity and witch-craft, which they may have inhaled while on the war path amongst a foreign tribe.

The Matabele retain likewise some strange notions regarding certain birds, beasts, and snakes, which have to do with witchcraft, and are looked upon as uncanny.

One bird, called by the natives *umtegwana*, whose haunts are in rivers and valleys, is the possessor of a powerful charm, and because of this it is never shot or killed, for they say you cannot shoot that bird and live. A white man, not knowing this superstition, shot one not very far from my house. A native who saw this, some months after, asked me very solemnly if that white man was still alive who shot the medicine bird ; and when told that he was, remarked, ' You must have given him some powerful medicine to counteract that of the bird, which but for your interference would have killed him.'

The ant-bear is a dangerous beast. To see one,

WITCHCRAFT AND RAIN-MAKING.   47

according to native belief, is nothing short of a sad calamity. It is never killed, unless by the chief's special orders, its flesh being used on certain important occasions as medicine.

The owl, of which there are several species, is a witch of no mean order, and is hated very much, partly on account, they say, of its glaring eyes, and of its midnight meandering in the towns. If it happens to light on the top of a hut, the inmates, if suspected of witchcraft, will go at once and report this to the chief.

Another bird, a small wood pigeon, must not be killed by stones or clubs, or else all your calves will sicken and die; but if you catch it by means of a trap and kill it, no evil follows.

The feathers and flesh of the king eagle are used by the chief, and contain medicinal properties, which have power over the clouds and cause it to rain.

No one dare shoot a crocodile (a man was killed not long ago for this, he wanted some part of it for bewitching), without a special permit from the chief, for its liver is supposed to be a very powerful factor in the list of almost numberless ingredients required in the process of making rain. You may shoot one in the winter, but not during the rainy season.

The hippopotamus has also some particular function in this connection.

The wolf, as we have already seen, is one of the witches that roam about at night seeking whom they may devour.

Snakes, it need scarcely be said, play an important

part in many heathen countries, for they are associated with witchcraft, and contain charms of all kinds, even the spirits of the departed. There are two distinct classes of snakes in Matabeleland, the evil and the good.

Witch doctors go hunting certain species among the hills—there are no snake-charmers in the land—the skins of which they tie round their waists; and the bones of which they convert into a necklace, which they also wear on high occasions. I asked a witch-doctor once whom I met if he had been away hunting men, or witches, or what? 'No, I have been among the hills after snakes,' he said, 'whose skins, bones, and medicines I am very much in need of.'

The natives tell me certain snakes contain the spirits of their ancestors; these do not bite, and are perfectly harmless; they are the spirit snakes,[1] and are allowed to go about their huts, and are not feared or killed by the people. But if you press them for a practical illustration, by asking them to take hold of any particular one by their hand, then they smile in a way that gives you the impression this is mere talk about the *Inyoka wamadhozi*, the spirit snakes not biting if they had the opportunity. This much at all events one may safely state—that the experiment has never been attempted. The people dread and will not touch a dead snake, far less a live one. If you tell them to throw a dead snake away, they pick it up on their kerry and cast it away from them with a shout of fear and disgust, and afterwards

---

[1] But there is also a biting poisonous one, which in their view contains a wicked spirit, and has a spite against you.

take ashes or earth and clean that part of their club on which the snake rested.

There are certain notions about snakes, to the effect that they have to do with rain-making, good harvests, the sickness of man and beast, the being fortunate and unfortunate. The chief uses various species in making rain. Several large skins, fifteen or sixteen feet long, may be seen hanging on the fence of his brick enclosure, where he does most of his performances just before the commencement of the season. Crocodile skins, birds' skins, hippopotami heads, roots, leaves, and bones of all kinds, shapes and sizes are brought out, put down on the ground and used for the purpose of rain-making.

The largest snake I ever saw and shot was between seven and eight feet long; it killed one of my hens in my yard. Once we killed another three feet long in our bedroom; and several others have suffered death at our hands. It has been seldom in my experience that people have died from a snake bite; all who have been doctored by us for it have recovered. But my experience of snakes is not altogether pleasant, as the following incident will show. Happening to be in a native town once, when a large green snake made its appearance, I joined in the hunt after it. People came from all quarters, running with clubs, sticks, and spears in their hands to kill the witch. It was quite an exciting time; it disappeared underneath the overlapping thatch of the hut. In stooping down to look where it had gone, all at once I felt something as if it had been several drops of water going into my eyes, which set them on fire, for it was a poisonous fluid emitted from the snake's mouth. The pain was intense for some time. The people gathered round me, expressing their sympathy, saying what a pity I had been bewitched in the eyes, for I would never see any more; I was in ill-luck, and all the rest of it. However, on reaching home, I applied medicine, and my eyes were all right next day, to the great astonishment of everybody in that town.

I was told of one man who was besieged by five snakes coming straight for him while sitting in his hut, all of which he killed. Some days after, other six appeared, which he declared came for the purpose of bewitching him. He fled the country, and became very sick, but returned home some months afterwards.

A GROUP OF MATABELE AND OTHER WARRIORS.

CHAPTER IV.

ARTS AND CRAFTS.

ONE of the most popular professions, because the most lucrative, is that of the *isanusi* or *witch-doctor*. Many young men every year leave their regiments and become witch-doctors. The voice of the witch-doctor is often that of the chief. His sole work is to find out who has killed cattle or people, blighted the crops, chased the rain away, brought sickness, or, indeed, who is the person, guilty or not, who shall be accused as the cause of any of a hundred other troubles that may come upon the people.

Zondo is the greatest in this profession, being the oldest one in the country, whose history may be briefly stated here. Chaka wished to test his wise men, and did so after this fashion. Two slaves were ordered to kill several cattle in his kraal. Next morning, on going there, he professed to be thunderstruck at finding them speared and dead. The witch-doctors were all called, among whom was this Zondo, whose verdict after much noise and talking was that they were killed by a certain man, who possessed much cattle. At this Chaka gave command to his soldiers to kill all witch-doctors, but some of them escaped, and Zondo was one of them. He journeyed northward with Umzilikazi, and is now one of the oldest men living in the country. His son has taken up this profession ; and many besides are occupying their time in practising it among the tribe.

But there are different forms or kinds of occupation to which the name doctor is applied. The title is applied to those who deal in roots and leaves and barks of trees, and who are known as medical men ; to those who are known as rain-doctors ; to those who have the arranging of the annual war-dance, who are called the dance-doctors ; to interpreters of the cause of sicknesses, and to interpreters of dreams ; to those who consecrate a site on which a new town is going to be built ; and to those who preside at the ceremony of the first fruits. The *bone-thrower* is not known exactly as a doctor, though they often talk of him as such. But there is yet another who doctors the soil in the gardens before they begin to dig and sow the Kaffir corn, mealies, beans, and pumpkins. All these may be *izinyana* doctors, but to distinguish the fine differences between them is beyond my ken. Only let me add that scarcely a single week passes without some one being hunted up by these black-robed fiends, and every month of the year nine or ten suffer death at their hands. These wizards, whose hearts are full of cruelty and whose feet run to shed innocent blood, receive oxen and sheep from the people ; and are often bribed to bring false charges against the man who has a few more oxen than his neighbours. Many happy homes are thus broken up for ever, and human life is dragged down into the thick mud and abominations of heathenism. This

tracking of the guilty, or of those accused, is called
'smelling out.'

In order to join this smelling-out fraternity, the
following process must be enacted. You wander
about in the veldt all alone, singing, yelling, and
shouting; you refuse food, eat no beans; you jump
about at home, put on any amount of 'side,' until
your friends go and inform the king that your
intention is to be an *isanusi*. He orders you to go
to several of the craft, who test your smelling-out
ability. If they are satisfied, then they give you
certain medicines to drink, tie some snake's bones
round your neck, and one or two skins round your
waist, and decorate your head with blown-up goat's
entrails. These are your degree robes, which you
wear when trying a case. You live by yourself, may
have one or two wives, a few servants, a garden, and
a small flock of sheep and goats.

Another occupation in which many are engaged is
that of the blacksmith, and an important and useful
one it is too in the country. A blacksmith is a man
of influence and is respected by the tribe, for it is he
who is the man of iron, who makes their picks, axes,
and spears. Let us follow him through the whole
process of spear-making.

His first business, then, is to gather his ironstone,
of which there is any quantity all over the land, and
smelt it, which he does in a clay pot, in which he puts
first a layer of coke, then one of ironstone, and so on
alternately, until it is filled. The lid is another
broken pot on the top of this one, and all the cracks
are smeared up with clay and cow-dung. The pot

clay furnace is rested upon three stones, underneath which a fire of sticks is kept up night and day until the ironstone is smelted. The bellows with which he blows consists of two leathern bags or sacks made out of goatskins. To the neck end of each sack is attached a wooden tube or ox horn, which again communicates with another tube made of clay, which is inserted into the fire. At the top of this bellows-sack is another hole, round the edges of which are

A MATABELE BLACKSMITH.

fixed two or three short thin sticks, which form what is called the handle of the bellows. Now these two sacks are put close together, with just enough room for a person to sit between them, and with one in each hand he lifts them up alternately, not off the ground, only the length of the sack, and on their being pressed down again a steady current of air passes out through the wooden tube and horn into

ARTS AND CRAFTS.

the fire. The smelting process over, a flat stone which serves as an anvil is brought, and with another small one which he uses as a hammer he beats his iron into the shape of a pick, or a spear, or a bangle for the wrist or leg, or whatever he wants to make. If the iron is too hot to hold in his hand, he uses a pair of native-made nippers or a mealy cob, into which he presses the one end of the iron while he pounds the other with his stone hammer. He repairs half-worn native picks; and when we remember his primitive mode of working, it is surprising how well he can make spears and axes.

The people of Demu, a subdued tribe, paid tribute every year to Lobengula in picks alone, and their specimens of ironwork are very creditable indeed. I asked a blacksmith to make me a spear out of an old bolt once, but he refused by saying that our iron was too poor to be flattened out; but he brought me several made from native iron ore, and I must say no English blacksmith could have made them more straight, neat, or graceful. The number of people engaged in this useful art is very limited compared to those who have adopted the witchcraft profession.

In every large town there are *war-shield cutters* whose special work it is to prepare and take care of this highly valued implement of war. There are really two distinct shields, though both are made out of specially prepared ox-hide. Cow-hides are not used for making war-shields, only ox-hides. The one kind of shield is much smaller than the other, has a different name, and is used by herd-boys in the veldt and those who go visiting their friends, buying corn, or who are sent on messages by the chief. The war shield proper is never used except on special occasions, such as going on impi, at the annual war-dance, or when the men dance before the king, in what may be called a review of his soldiers, or when ten or fifteen are sent to murder a supposed witch. Most of these shields are made from skins of oxen. An ox-skin is put in the river at sunset; next day about eight o'clock it is taken by several men and washed clean all over in the water; after which it is placed in the cattle kraal underneath the dung and thoroughly softened. Wooden mallets are used in beating it till it is pliable, when it is cut into shield shape, four or five feet long, and about two at the widest point in the middle. It is oval shaped, the hairy side is the outside, and inside a long stick is fixed, the top end of which is decorated with the tail of a wild cat wrapped round it. Right along the middle, longways, little holes are cut, through which another piece of soft hide, but of different colour, is drawn. A small handle allows two fingers to grasp it. Sometimes three or four spears will be fastened inside by the stick. A man who is able to cut out a war shield in proper shape—he has no measure or line to guide his knife—is considered to be highly gifted, is in fact a genius among his friends and neighbours. The shield is carried in the left hand; the lower part of it strikes the knee. The different regiments are known by the colour of the shields they carry.

The tailor, or he who sews the *war dresses*, is another person of some note among them. His head-dress, part of which covers the shoulders, is the most

MATABELE WEAPONS.

artistic piece of personal decoration in the country. It consists of picked, short black ostrich feathers. The one ambition of a young warrior is to possess one of these war-dress hoods. It is very expensive, and highly valued and much admired by everybody. One pound, or one and a quarter, of feathers will make a very good hood, provided they are all one colour. For these feathers you can buy a good ox. This hood is sewn together by means of certain rushes, which are twisted up into the shape of a cord, on which the feathers are fastened, and formed into the size to fit the individual who wears it. It takes about three days to make one of these hoods; and the one which was made for me cost two pounds of beads only. Many are engaged in this profession, and are appreciated for their work's sake. Many work for years before they are able to gather together sufficient feathers to make a hood. They buy a few here with calico or beads or with a goat, and walk for days in another direction after the hunting season to seek elsewhere until they have enough. The war-hood is preserved in an earthen vessel hermetically sealed, which is put away carefully and looked after as if it were full of the most precious pearls of the ocean. One lasts for years; but it often happens that during the days of the dance it rains continually, and the wet spoils the beauty of this artistic arrangement of feathers, which above all other things except oxen is most highly prized and jealously guarded by the Matabele.

Next we mention the *wood carver*, who makes spoons, wooden dishes, and several-sized vases with lids, which are used for holding thick milk during the summer season. The spoons they sup with, while the dishes they require for holding beef, carrying corn, drinking purposes, and as bowls from which they eat the Kaffir corn porridge. Certain long spoons are made for stirring the beer-pot. These carved utensils are bought and sold among the people themselves. There are no idols carved by them, nor ornaments seen in their low-doored smoky dwellings. The chief has all his meat served up to him in wooden dishes, while his beer is drunk out of European tin dishes.

Others again, mostly women, are engaged in *basket making*. There are large baskets used in beer-brewing and in harvest-time, small ones for winnowing the corn, carrying it on their heads, and other uses besides. Special small finely-made baskets are sewn and used as beer-tankards. Some of these, with little beautifully made lids, look very neat and nice, and are strong for many years' wear and tear. Many old women who cannot do anything else make baskets, so also do the old queens.

But another thing they make also is *mats*, on which they lie at night, with a wooden block carved after a new moon shape, to serve as a pillow. These mats look very pretty sometimes, and much labour is spent on them. The floor of their huts is hard, and sometimes shining; they put these mats down, and on them lie the poorer classes, with an ox-hide pounded soft on the top of them.

There are two other important occupations, and these are gardening and taking care of the oxen, goats, and sheep. They work in their gardens six months of the year, and there most of the women and girls find employment. During the winter all the cattle and sheep are removed to the outskirts of the country, where there is good grass and plenty of it. They are away from three to four months—from September till December. A goodly number are employed by the chief in going to and fro with messages, medicines, and presents to those who are in his favour, whom he believes to have power to make rain. Keeping the huts in repair, removing to new sites every few years, and digging the chief's gardens—these also constitute occupations.

Beyond this narrow limit the Matabele know little or nothing; the civilised world, throbbing with life, is to them as if it were not. But in recent years there have been signs of change. Many go to the white people seeking employment, and return with new ideas of life, duty, and work. They wake up to find that they are men capable of earning money, goods, and property. Besides this, they also see how insecure is everything they possess. The disposition to work and be independent grows among the people; and the wholesale butchery of families and towns, which is still a most common occurrence, tends to increase their desire for liberty. Even among these savages are those who desire freedom from the terrible witchcraft which reigns, to enjoy what has been earned by the sweat of their brow.

I leave this subject with one more word—namely, that the great majority of the Matabele proper are occupied chiefly in the destruction of one another for jealousy and revenge.

Some thirty years ago trading was a very different matter from what it is at the present day. Then, in the 'good old days,' you could buy from the natives a sheep for a few beads, an ox for a strip of calico, and an elephant's tusk of ivory for a snuff-box. Besides, tiger-skins were cheap, as were all other wild animals' skins, and the intrinsic value of ostrich-feathers was known only by white men. These articles formed the principal trade on the part of the natives, and they form the principal part to-day, with this exception, perhaps, that there are more oxen, while there is less ivory for sale. After the occupation of Mashonaland by white men the chief entered into contracts with certain trading and gold companies, which paid him a sum of something like £2,000 per annum, which money was his alone, the nation as such having nothing whatever to do with it. Perhaps up to the outbreak of the war the most important business done with the natives was in buying cattle. Sometimes difficulties arose in this connection; but it is matter of regret that so little business was carried on in the land. Had the people been brought more into contact with respectable white men trading all over the country, it might have produced a very salutary effect. For a long time the one store at Bulawayo was oftener empty than full of barter goods. The natives do not deal in money, though now and then some who had been away working at Johannesburg and Kimberley brought a little to buy with. Waggons came at uncertain intervals. There was no regular system of bartering. What is one waggon-load of barter stuff when it is spread over 15,000 natives who have things for sale? It is finished, sold out and done with in a day or two. A thoroughgoing business, if established, would require its warehouses to be kept full of goods. On the road there should be a rolling stock constantly on the waggon-wheels moving on towards Bulawayo. Blankets and rugs of divers colours, red, white, and blue, yellow, pink, and black, varying in price from 5s. to 25s. each, would be welcomed. Clothing also is purchased, moleskin and corduroy, thick, coarse, and strong, in suits; but there should be fifty pairs of trousers to every hundred of coats and waistcoats. Hats and waistcoats are at a discount, having been very much used as presents among the natives. This remark also applies to knives, small and great, to snuff-boxes, tinder-boxes, shirts, and common brass chains. Guns and ammunition are always in demand. Powder in flasks is preferred to that in bags.

Beads also are in request. The prime colours most liked are pink, black, blue, red and white eye, white alone, yellow (royal colour), pink striped, blue striped. If you like to bring large gaudy coloured beads for the queens you may, but those just mentioned are most used in trading with the natives. They must be a certain size, about so (o) big. If the red white eye are a little larger so much the better.

Calicoes are more in demand than any other kind of goods. During a year of hunger there were nearly 3,000 pieces sold at the small store at Bulawayo within three months' time, and there would have been as many more if they had been there for sale. The three principal colours in calicoes are black, white, and what is called cluster yellow with white spots. None of this class should cost more than threepence per yard at Manchester. A stiff strong calico is not suitable; it must be soft to the touch, as most of it is tied round the waists for show. Recent events have changed the outlook, but these notes of one for some years resident in the country may still have an interest. There has been a natural hesitancy in laying out large sums of money in a land where so far there has been no security.

Conceit and craftiness are two of the most prominent features in the character of the Matabele tribe. Self-satisfied, proud, and boastful of their past dark history, they disdain the idea of coming under, or asking for, the protection of any other nation, be it black or white. 'We, the mighty warriors of the great chief Umzilikazi, the sound of whose war-shield has struck terror and fear into the hearts of all his enemies'—they say in spirit—'we, the brave soldiers of the king of heaven, who never fled in battle, we need no protection, not from the most daring foe upon earth. Perish for ever the cowardly slave who ever uttered such a mean word! The white people may think us nothing, but we know we are brave and valiant in battle. Our enemies have fallen before our spear, our land is ours by right of conquest. If any other nation conquers us we will submit, but to beg and cringe like a slave for protection is what we will never do.' This is the Zulu spirit of the older people, which at the measureless expense of human life clings tenaciously to the old order of things, and is opposed to all progress. It will accept certain germs of civilisation, but it ignores and despises to the utmost its laws and liberties. This spirit of self-confidence is most marked among the older indunas, headmen, and queens, and all who are related to or are distant cousins of the present chief. Amongst this class it is no exaggeration to say that their conceit is like their country, it has no bounds. It is in their eyes boundless.

The very carriage and bearing of the people indicate their conceited spirit; their condescending way of speaking to you shows it; their manner, talk and impudence are quite enough to prove it. They are too conceited to prefer the plough to their picks in tilling their gardens. The chief may have one, a waggon too, and a chair to sit upon, but they would not deign to have any such things.

Their mode of address is sometimes very annoying. They may come upon you when you are all alone and say, 'Halloo, white man, where are you going, where have you come from, what are you seeking in our country? Who gave you permission to come here? Give us a present or we will take your hat. You are nobody. Don't you know we are the young soldiers of the king? Don't you see our dress, our sticks, spears, and shields? We will thrash you if you don't give us a *tusa*.' This is something after their style of talking, especially if you are alone and they are ten or fifteen in number. But to read these words is quite a different thing from seeing them acted in the different expressions of face, and tone of voice, and threatening attitude, which they assume in front of you, as you walk along the footpath.

This spirit overrules justice and equality. A proud conceited Matabele, if he has the ear of the chief, has no scruples if it suits his purpose in putting a slave to death. It does happen now and then that some one of the upper circle is killed on account of witchcraft; but for one of high birth, ten of low birth become the victims of injustice and lies. The only court of appeal is the chief, and it is just as likely as not that the victim of a false charge or of any wrong may receive no redress of any kind, even if his case is proved beyond the shadow of a doubt.

In craftiness, downright craftiness, my opinion is that they cannot be beaten. Craft is born and trained in the perpetual warfare and struggle of savage life. Naturally they are suspicious of one another, ever on the alert. They always walk about with their clubs and spears in their hands. Their words are never to be depended upon, and they will tell you the greatest lies, merely for the sake of talking, but more often with a view of trying to get you to give them a present. They come professing to be sick, while all the while they are asking you for medicine for some one else. Without giving you the least possible hint they will sell you sick sheep and goats, or cattle that have been stolen. In buying Kaffir corn also you must be on your guard, for often they put good corn in the mouth of the bag while at the bottom it is old, weevil-eaten, mixed with earth and stone, and not fit for food. Once

ARTS AND CRAFTS.

when travelling to Tati my oxen that were grazing in the bushes quite near by, while we were having our mid-day meal, were driven by some young fellows who were out hunting through one of their gardens, with the express purpose of getting some calicoes and beads out of me. All of a sudden they came rushing up to the waggon, shouting, 'Pay us for our corn; your oxen have finished our garden, none is left, hunger will kill us. Pay us the damage, or else we will take two of your oxen from you.' I was helpless, and there was no way out of the difficulty but to pay and settle the matter, which I did with beads and calicoes. Having thus robbed me of my few things, they thought themselves very clever. Sufficient has been related to show how great is the need of caution in all dealings. One thing you must never do, and that is to break your word to them. They are close observers of character, and quick at reading you; but firmness and good temper and patience can do much even among such a people.

There is no word for time in their language, and it is the part and lot of dogs and slaves to hurry and work. Many white men who have lived there will bear me out when I say that if you hurry a black man anywhere in South Africa, you are bound to make less speed than if you took it quietly and steadily. The proverb holds good beyond a doubt, that the more you hurry the less speed you will make.

CHAPTER V.

THE WAR-DANCE AND THE FIRST FRUITS.

AT the time of the annual war-dance their large enclosure is well adapted for dancing purposes, being covered with a thick carpet of strong green grass, which feels soft and pleasant to the bare feet that dance on it. Bulawayo being the principal town, the great war-dance is held there. It is so called from the very warlike appearance of all the warriors, young and old, who assemble there from all parts of the country.

The country is marked out in five different divisions, with separate names, which need not be mentioned here, and each of these supplies so many head of cattle for slaughtering. Each regiment builds for itself small huts made of short sticks and grass, and occupies its own patch of ground just outside the town, and is known by the colour of its ox-hide shields. Each general is responsible for the behaviour of his men during the festive season.

The dress of the men on this occasion is very picturesque, and displays to perfection the peculiar though not ungraceful gait of the 'noble savage.' On his forehead and pointing upwards is a long crane feather, fixed there by means of a bow of otter skin which ties at the back, while on the crown of the head is a huge

THE WAR-DANCE AND THE FIRST FRUITS. 71

black tassel of beautiful short black ostrich feathers; and on the shoulders and half-way down the chest is a hood of the same. This is the most graceful part of the uniform of the men. Half way down their arms and legs ox-tail hair is tied, mostly white, while round their waists are hanging all sorts of skins—monkey, tiger, cat, rock rabbit; and above them, calicoes—spotted, striped black, yellow, and white. Add to this the large war shield in his left hand, and spear in his right, and there the Matabele stands—the proudest invincible warrior who ever served a king.

These all dance in a semicircle in the large enclosure, and within this again the girls and queens dance. All have sticks in their right hands, from three to nine feet long. Among the girls and queens pink beads, yellow beads, blue and spotted calicoes prevail. The blue jay birds' feathers are stuck fantastically in the heads of all the queens, some of whom wear long kilts of black and pink beads down to their knees, while others tie round their bodies pieces of spotted calico in all sorts of ways. They all sing the same song at one time, march slowly forward, and keep time to their song by stamping on the ground. The hand with the long thin switch goes up and down according to the music. The girls from the towns sing abreast, while the queens come out from their quarters in single file. The men have short sticks with little knobs at the ends. No spears are used on this occasion.

This great feast lasts for four or five days, its real object being to thank the chief, who prays to the spirits of his ancestors for the gift of fresh corn, and food, and to show their loyalty by singing his praises. Many have ulterior objects in going to this dance, such as eating beef and drinking beer.

Between each dance the Matabele count twelve moons, so that it is really their Christmas festival, and takes place between the end of December and February. If the rains are early, the time will be altered accordingly. Before the time messengers are sent out to bid the people to the feast, and they come as we have seen, and gather each regiment by itself outside Bulawayo.

During all these ceremonies no business of any kind is done; no waggon dares leave the town while the dance is going on. The chief is relieved of his duties, he does not rule; the doctors of the dance—the masters of the ceremonies—have all the power, and they give orders about the time it is to be, and their orders are obeyed. On the first day of the dance, when everybody has arrived, the important business is the handing over to the chief of the number of oxen which have been brought from the different towns throughout the country. These are all numbered and handed over to the chief inside his kraal, as an offering from the people to the spirits of his ancestors. The cattle are carefully shut up in the kraal all night; and on the second day the slaughtering begins. At early dawn all the army is up and singing the war songs outside the cattle kraal, while the chief and his head priest are inside selecting the oxen which are to be slain. Here the chief offers up his prayer. Here so-and-so takes this ox. The chief points out a certain number, and the dance doctor, who is skilled in spearing cattle, soon has all his victims groaning on the ground. None are killed outside the gate; all must fall within. There is no choosing as to colour or size, only they must be speared by the priest. He spears each one behind the left shoulder; some stand minutes afterwards, others drop immediately, and are soon dead.

No one may go inside the kraal during this operation, but when it is completed the command goes forth to skin the cattle. The singing of war songs, which has been going on outside all this time, now ceases, and there is a regular stampede of men with knives of all descriptions running here, there, and everywhere. So many oxen, perhaps sixty, eighty, or a hundred, have been slain, and each regiment receives its number, and sets about skinning them at once. There is no confusion, for each man knows where he has to go and what he has to do.

The skinning over, the meat is halved, quartered, and cut up, and made ready to be carried away to one or more huts, in which it is piled up in heaps for the night, for the spirits of the chief's ancestors to come and eat their share first of all. This day none are allowed meat of any kind except the feet, tails, and entrails of the oxen.

The third day the singing and dancing continue. The excitement grows more intense towards afternoon, when the chief appears in full war dress himself, and throws a spear from the gate of the kraal into the enclosure where all the people are. At this point the shouting, yelling, and tumult are something awful. They come gradually closer and closer, right to within a few yards of the kraal gate, to have a sight of his majesty. Many, most of them in fact, are crowded out as they approach the gate; the crush is frightful; and if the wind is blowing from them towards you it is not pleasant. They rush on to get near the gate, and then fall back again a hundred yards or so from it.

At early morn, after the spirits have had their feed, the beef is all taken from the huts and put in earthenware pots, some fifty or sixty of them. It remains cooking all day, the pots being covered with broken pieces of others, and smeared with cowdung and set a-boiling.

Towards sunset the meat is taken out and handed round, the people all sitting down on the grass in the presence of the chief to enjoy their repast. No knives are used on this occasion; they use their teeth only, and the meat is handed round from man to man until they have all had a share.

Next day they may continue their dancing; but this feast over, they soon disperse and go to their own homes. There are various favourite dances, such as the corn dance, at the end of which each one points towards his garden with his stick. There is, too, the dance of the sharp-pointed spear, to which the words are sung: 'Come and see, hear the news!' 'What news?' 'The news of the spear, the mighty spear of the great king!'

On the fourth day the dance is practically ended; and between this and reaping-time there is nothing for the people to do but sit and plot and plan for one another's death. It is in these months that so many are killed for witchcraft.

After this annual festival the chief as a rule leaves Bulawayo for his other country mansions, perhaps Emkanweni, Ingujeni, or Umvujwa, which are within a radius of six miles of the large town. He travels in an ox-waggon driven by his own 'boys.'

Beside the great war-dance, there is an annual ceremony of the first fruits. No one dare for his life eat any green food, such as mealies, or sweet reeds, before observing this ceremony. It takes place just immediately after the big dance. The principal towns *luma*, *i.e.* bite, first, and those in the outlying districts follow. I went as an eye-witness to see this ceremony performed at a neighbouring town among the hills.

There are special doctors set apart for the occasion. The smaller villages gather together to the larger ones. I remember on my arrival seeing the doctor busy preparing his medicines in front of the people, who were arranged before him in the cattle kraal in a semicircle. In their hands were no shields or spears, only short sticks, which was a sign that they were about to perform or observe a custom of peace.

As I sat down the master of the ceremony rose and took a wooden dish in which were some green leaves of *makomani*—a kind of vegetable marrow—and clean water. This he put on the ground in close proximity to the people, who were all dancing and chanting a song. A giraffe's tail tied on a short stick was in his hand, which he dipped into this dish several times. Then he sprinkled the people. Returning to where I was sitting, he greeted me and expressed pleasure at seeing me there to witness the performance.

Just in front of him were some sweet reed-stalks, *makomani*, and pumpkin leaves, and two small bags full of medicines, which consisted of the usual native miscellaneous collection of snakes' skins, and bones, feathers of wild birds, bones of wild animals, twigs and leaves of various trees. A log of wood was brought, and with his small axe he chopped off from each of his bundles of 'medicine,' roots, bones and skins a little bit. These pieces he gathered together in a heap on a sheep skin, which was put there close by for that purpose.

Two fires were now lit, and a native earthenware pot was brought and balanced on three stones, while under it was the fire. A second pot, which was broken, was used to form a lid. Into the sound pot were put all the leaves and sweet reed, and where the two pots met was smeared some cowdung, to prevent the steam from getting out. Another broken pot was used in cooking up all the chips of roots, bits of feathers, and splinters of bones, but no lid was put on it. Fortunately for me, the wind was blowing the smoke towards the people, who all this time were chanting their dirges about forty yards away.

Four reeds about three feet long were fetched and laid down beside this smoking broken pot in which was this smouldering, smelling concoction of roots and bones. At a given signal four men from the ranks approach on hands and knees towards this reeking, smoky mass. Each one picks up one of the reeds, one end of which he puts in his mouth and the other

THE WAR-DANCE AND THE FIRST FRUITS. 77

into the thickest part of this stinking smoke; and with this he sucks one mouthful of smoke from the pot into his mouth, then he puffs it into the air, lays down the reed, spits once or twice on the ground, and returns again to his singing. This they all do in batches of four in turns, till each one has tasted the wonderful cleansing power of the doctor's medicine. The ashes are afterwards taken out of this old broken vessel and put on a flat stone, and by means of another round one are ground into fine dust, not unlike charcoal.

Next they brought a dishful of warm milk from a white cow, which was poured into this vessel, out of which the ashes had been taken; and when the milk began to boil, the officiating 'doctor' threw back into it all this black charcoal-looking stuff, together with some white dust which made a perfume, and stirred them all up by means of a long stick. As soon as this second potful of ingredients was cooked sufficiently, the singing ceased, and the people all stood staring at this white frothy substance of which they were about to partake. They again came forward, but instead of using reeds they used their fingers, by dipping them into the hot milk and next putting them into their mouths. This was repeated three or four times by them all, when they moved away to their singing place again.

Attention was then directed to the other pot, which had the broken pot for a lid, and in which were the sweet reeds and vegetable marrow leaves which had been brought fresh from their gardens that morning. The lid was taken off, and all these leaves were eaten up by the people; only the stalks on which the leaves grow were brought back, together with the husks and the remainder of the charcoal stuff, chips and splinters, and put in the fire and all burned up, not a shred of any being left after the ceremony was over. While eating these green leaves the people strike themselves on their head, elbows, and knees, signifying thereby that by means of this young crop —first fruits of the new season—they desire to be strong in head, arms and limbs, to fight the chief's battles.

To complete the performance, the priest, with his giraffe's tail brush sprinkles them a second time with this milky charcoal substance, saying to them all the while, 'Now you have observed the law of the land; now your offering has been given and your songs sung. Go and eat the first fruit of your gardens; go eat, be filled and rejoice.' This is all; they disperse and the ceremony ends.

It ought to be added that, previous to their congregating for this purpose, the people go at early dawn to wash themselves in the river. There is no hard-and-fast line regarding the age of the individual, from twelve or fifteen years perhaps they begin to observe the ceremony. Only men and youths go through it; no women are allowed to be present, though they may look on from a distance. If one is from home at such a time, or unable to attend through sickness, some friend of his will take to him part of this leaf of vegetable marrow, which is mixed or soaked with the priest medicine. He eats it, and is thereby cleansed and fit to eat the green food of the season. It would be saying too much if we affirmed that this rule is observed by everybody. Many, in fact, long before this ceremony takes place are so pinched with hunger that they must eat the green food of their gardens or die; while others are specially privileged in this way by asking permission from the chief, who is the first to *luma* the green food of the season. Even before this public act he may have been enjoying nice green cabbages and fresh potatoes from his own garden.

CHAPTER VI.

MATABELE WOMEN AND CHILDREN.

As in all heathen countries, the women are the drudges of the men, so is this true in a special sense in this land. Let us follow a woman through her duties, and find out what is her position and influence among the Matabele. In the first place, she is a hewer of wood and a carrier of water. When cold, drizzly days come, and rain falls, she has to provide the wood for the fire and cooking purposes. When beer brewing is a-going, and it is pretty frequent after a good harvest of Kaffir corn, thirty or forty young girls start at early dawn for the distant hills, perhaps six miles away, with axes and bark twine to gather sticks to cook the beer with. In our district they gather mostly wild olive wood from the gorges of the hills; this contains resin, makes a nice flame, burns well, and has a black smoke not unlike the smoke of coal. They walk on a narrow footpath, the one behind the other, in a long single file, singing as they go scampering along, which outwardly at least gives you the impression that in some measure they are happy and free. The whole responsibility of providing water rests upon the woman, and it has to be carried sometimes two miles from the river, though in the rainy season it is found in pools and fountains near by. The earthen pots that hold it, made by herself out of pot-clay which abounds in the valleys, are carried on her head. On a small ring made of grass, or leaves, she steadies the water-pot, but many carry it on their bare heads without protection of any kind. The wonder is how she is able to support a jar of thirty or forty pounds' weight, and carry it all these long distances up steep hills, on rugged and stony footpaths, on her head. I never saw a man carry a water-pot on his head. There is a sharp line drawn between the work allotted to the men and the work of the women. As long as the men are occupied in war or in hunting, it seems an inevitable division of labour, but in times of idleness the men would still count it degradation to have any part in these tasks.

When spring time comes all the young girls who cannot help in the gardens stay at home to take care of the little children. Their gardens are in size from one acre to six acres in extent, but their size and number very much depend on whether a man may have two, or four, or six wives. Most of the indunas have five or six wives, so also the chief's relatives, and men of high birth. Many mothers, with their little babies tied on their backs by means of a brayed goat or sheep skin, dig all their gardens alone. When tired of holding their wee bairns, they put them down by the edge of the garden to play while they go on digging. It baffles one to understand how these poor little ones can endure the burning rays of the hot tropical sun, which comes pouring down upon their unprotected heads. Just at this time—the digging

G

season—the natives themselves say 'the sun burns.' It is not merely hot, but its heat is at burning point. Where friendly shady trees are near the garden the children play there, and where there are not any, leafy branches are cut down, and a temporary shade is fixed in the garden as a protection from the burning sun.

This sowing time, during October and November, is often very trying for the women; for if they have sown their garden, and the rain delays its coming, or it falls at long intervals, then their labour is lost, the seed dies from the heat of the sun, and they have to sow a second time, in hopes of reaping a harvest in June or July. In this digging of the gardens all help who can, from the queens downward. The men, too, take a share in the work, and everybody is busy.

If any one has corn with which to brew thirty gallons of beer, he calls a digging match, and some twenty or thirty people will come and work for him. They drink the beer and dig the garden at the same time. There is much time spent in connection with this beer-brewing business. All the chief's beer—and that is not a small quantity, when you remember that there are always some thirty or forty wives with him to drink it—is carried to him by women and girls in large calabashes from long distances of twenty to forty miles. At the great annual war dances, hundreds of calabashes are consumed. Again, when you ask who makes all this beer, the answer is, the women.

If before her marriage a woman in this land is a drudge and a slave, she is much more so after it. Her husband, as a rule, is a lazy, exacting, indolent man, whose chief business is talking about wars, capturing slaves and cattle, and hunting wild animals. As a rule, the woman digs and watches the garden, fetches wood and water, cooks for her husband and children, and thatches her own hut. If she has any spare time she makes baskets, and beautiful ones too, from reeds which grow in the valleys. A woman's proper place is her home, where her work is, and beyond which she has no influence whatever. The only woman to my knowledge who interfered in political affairs was the chief's own sister, whose name was Umncene, and who for this, or other reasons, was killed some ten years ago.

A woman, however, may visit her friends; she may carry her corn for sale to the white man's store, she may go to the war dance at Bulawayo. There is one thing she is not exempted from possessing—the supposed power to bewitch, on account of which she often suffers shame, persecution, and death. It often happens, moreover, that when her husband is suspected of witchcraft, if they kill him she will share his fate. On the other hand, if her husband die, and she is suspected of having to do with it, it is no uncommon thing for her to hang herself, or drown herself in the river, rather than be clubbed to death. There are a few aged women who enjoy a peaceful old age. Their relatives and friends provide huts and food for them, the two main things required in the tribe; as for clothing, well, a few old bucks' (goats) or sheep skins are all that is necessary.

Let me try and describe to you a Matabele woman's dress. Before marriage she wears a string of various colours of beads, pink and black being her favourite hues, round her neck, wrists, and ankles; earrings of berries, and brass buttons are used, while round her waist are several strings of beads, black or spotted calico tied fast, and a sheepskin in front and behind. From the waist upwards nothing is worn, except that on very cold days they enfold themselves in a soft brayed ox-hide. After marriage they receive a distinctive mark, which consists in a kilt-shaped piece of ox-hide, specially softened inside, whilst outside it is threaded out in small strings, smeared with fat and charcoal. There is also a distinguishing mark between the wife of a common *ring kop*—an ordinary man—and the wives (queens?) of the king, of whom there are over eighty. The royal wives are allowed to wear a small flat piece of clay, about the size of half-a-crown, on the crown of their heads, which is considered a mark of high honour, only conferred on those of the chief's own household. Finger rings are not very common among them; no nose or lip jewels are worn, nor is their hair pointed, plaited, and plastered over with red clay and grease, as with some of the neighbouring tribes. Their most fashionable colours are yellow (royal colour), pink, black, blue, white, and red, all of which are seen on their calicoes, blankets, and shawls. Necklaces of different colours, of beads and bracelets, too, are often worn, though most of the big large beads are only used by the 'upper ten,' who live round or near by the king.

Marriage is almost as often a matter of compulsion as consent on the part of the young woman, for it is a question of oxen with the father of the bride; it is a question of the highest bidder, and not one of selection or affection. I knew a young man who married one of the daughters of a white man in the country, and the next time the father paid a visit to headquarters the chief asked him how many oxen he had received.

Matabele mothers love their children. They carry their little ones long distances—twenty or thirty miles—for medicine ; and the children enjoy, in spite of their very imperfect sanitary arrangements, fairly good health.

Yet, sad to relate, the little innocent babe is not exempt from the supposed taint of witchcraft, and often is killed in cold blood along with its parents. A neighbour of mine fled the country, leaving behind a young lad, two wives, and two little infants, all of whom were butchered, having been suspected of being in league with their father.

The little ones, as soon as they can, crawl about in the clothes in which they were born ; they may have one string of beads round their waist or neck, but, as a rule, they wear nothing at all on their little bodies. Their toys consist of a few white pebbles and other stones, with which they make huts and sheep-folds on the ground; but their principal toy is pot-clay from the valley, with which they make for themselves mud oxen.

The child's first real work, if a boy, is herding sheep and goats, of which he is very proud. Perhaps one or two boys join together their flocks ; and while the sheep graze on the sloping hillside or broad valley, they with their little clubs and shields go a-hunting hares, and pheasants, and birds, at their own sweet will. They become expert at throwing their kerries, and not unfrequently bring down flying pheasants and partridges.

No boys of this age are ever taken with their parents to the chief, and very few go to the annual dance. From herding the sheep or goats the boy, when about twelve years old, is taken to herd the cattle, a much more responsible duty; and he is sent away with seventy, or eighty, or a hundred head to herd in the veldt. At early dawn, when he has assumed his new position, he is up with the sun, letting out the calves from their pole enclosure to join their mothers in the large one, which is encircled by the huts of the town. He, too, milks the cows, not into a pail, but into his mouth, for the milk is part and sometimes the only food he has when herding on the outskirts of the land during the dry season. Milk is otherwise of small consequence to the natives. Neither men nor women drink new milk; they use it when sour only, mixed and boiled up with bruised corn. The boys and lads only drink it fresh. The waste every year of good rich milk from their thousands of cows is beyond calculation.

During all this period of cattle herding, from about twelve years to sixteen or eighteen, the young lad's mind is filled with all kinds of heathen notions, the customs and the beliefs of his tribe and his position as to birth. He sits in the evenings listening to the stories of his elders; how they fought in battle, how they routed their enemies; stories full of excitement in hunting of lions, tigers, and elephants. He is told of the divine power of his chief, of his boundless domains, of his great father whose death is spoken of as the falling of a mountain. If he has grown up in the country, perhaps, before he is eighteen years of age, he is *buted*, called by the king along with five or six hundred others to form a new regiment. During the ten years of my residence among them five such regiments were called out by the chief and placed

A MATABELE YOUTH.

under military discipline. These warriors lived all by themselves. As soon as he arrives at this stage the lad imagines himself a soldier of no mean order: pride possesses him, and he hates all form of work; those who work for the white men are treated with contempt and hatred. He spends most of his time in collecting monkey and wild-cat skins, carving knob-kerries, making shields and spears. Hundreds and thousands have sometimes been thus employed. He comes to think that to be a bloodthirsty cruel savage of Matabele heathenism is the highest aim in life. What else beyond this does he know? Well, it ought to be added he may know how to fell trees with his native axe, to dig his garden with a native pick, and to skin an ox, or a sheep, or wild animal, to dance a few war songs, and sing them also, to the chant-like music peculiar to his race. After being in his regiment four or five years, he may marry one or more wives, and, unless engaged in raiding, may settle down to a life of inactivity, laziness, and uselessness. His wants are these: beer, porridge, beef occasionally, a blanket over his shoulders, a sheep and a cow, and a little tobacco.

The girl has, I think, a harder time of it, for she is mostly employed in looking after younger children, in work connected with the kraal, cooking, water-fetching, and so on. She is not so free in her childhood as the boy, and her future happiness, if there is such a thing in her life, greatly depends on her marriage. If she becomes the wife of a man who has already four or five others, I pity her. The constant quarrelling and biting of wives have no end, the petty jealousies and family broils are daily experiences. Also, the man and his wife may both belong to an induna, or some head man; and if this man who marries is not able to pay a given sum for his wife, then his children are not his—they are taken from him at the age of six or eight years, and he has no power to get them back again. Young captives who have cruel masters often run away to the white men, but in order to prevent them repeating the deed their little feet are burned, and in other ways they are punished by the merciless hand of heathenism. Others, who by neglect or accident allow the cattle or sheep into the gardens, often die from the results of an unmerciful beating. There being no example set before the young, they grow up just like unto their fathers, with their minds darkened, poisoned with vile superstitions, and all their attendant evils, while the little of civilisation they do see, and the family life of the missionaries, only impresses them with the idea that these ways are peculiar to the white people.

CHAPTER VII.

SICKNESS AND DEATH.

MALARIAL fever, contracted when out hunting, by sleeping in marshy swamps and low-lying districts, is common. There are numerous medicine men in the land who have some potent drugs, roots, leaves, berries, and barks of trees, and who doubtless give relief sometimes, though scores die yearly from the fever. Europeans may live in Matabele land, and never know what this fever is. There are eight or nine at least whom I know to have lived there for over ten years, and never to have been three consecutive days in bed. The country I consider is far ahead of Mashona land, or any other land south of the Zambesi, for purity of air, and adaptability for Europeans. Travel there, in the right season, build on the water-shed high land, live well, and with care you may not have one attack. The sound advice of one who lived most of his life in South Africa must not be forgotten : ' Have as much plain substantial food as possible, and eat as much of it as you can, *and eat regularly, and not by fits and starts.*' Men often get fever who are exposed to long fasts, whose system is in a low condition, who are careless and irregular in their meals, and who at the time of the first symptoms of fever have no nourishing food or medicine to check its rapid course, and the consequences are in such cases often fatal.

Many interesting cases of native sickness have come under my own notice; and here you touch the higher side of their heathen nature, and their thoughts are not always expressed in sound only, but in a tangible form. They would fain pay you with corn, mealies, hens, potatoes, goats, sheep, and oxen. One young man's father, after receiving benefit, brought a sheep unasked, and uttered the following: 'My friend, you have been good to me; my son you have brought back to life again; he is your child now, not mine. My heart is white towards you. I bring the best sheep in my wee flock as a thank-offering. Here it is; take it.' To read these words is one thing, to hear them spoken is quite another. That man meant what he said, for he felt it; he was grateful. Many instances could be mentioned of a similar nature, although help in various ways is rendered not for remuneration, but on the principle that each one here should be his brother's keeper.

Amongst the Matabele proper, and many others who have become incorporated into that tribe by conquest, it is firmly believed that all sickness, accidents, and death are the direct result of witchcraft. Yet they are very much like ourselves in cases of sickness and bereavement. What do they say, when they come to your place and find you ill with fever and unable to see them? They express themselves somewhat after this fashion: 'Sickness is a bad thing; it is ever with us; it is painful. What can we say when it comes? Who can prevent it

coming? We are helpless; no one can fight against
it. We don't know; we are silent for you. We don't
know; we don't know. You are troubled, and on
your account we are troubled also.' They speak
these words in a subdued quiet voice, as if they had
entered into your feelings; they also depart at once
from you, not to be in the way or cause disturbance
of any kind. To do so is to them sometimes a
great sacrifice. Some days after they may come
again to inquire how you are.

Death comes most frequently at the merciless
hands of witchcraft, in battle, or by old age. According to their moral standard, which is low and selfish
in the extreme, they believe in right and wrong, in a
future state, and in rewards and punishments. It is
often said by them that there are good and bad
white men, and good and bad black men. Their
language contains many words expressive of right
and wrong, good and evil, approval for doing good,
and punishment for wrong-doing. When a good
man dies, according to their idea of goodness, all
his relatives and friends come together to cry for
him, that is, bewail his death. Every one, man and
woman and child, come out of their huts, stamp up
and down their yards, wailing and yelling at the
pitch of their voice. It is a heart-rending sight,
which once seen can never be forgotten. With hands
clasped tightly together, and pressed between their
knees in a stooping posture, they shout and wail
and cry. *Aya, Ma! Mo! Um tanani*, if a child;
Baba wami, if a father; *Mama wami*, if a mother;
Omne wami, if a brother. To write these words,

SICKNESS AND DEATH.

which carry the burden of heart-felt weeping, means nothing; to hear them uttered is thrilling. I am not a sentimentalist, but have not been able to help being affected when in the midst of such a scene. Should any one join in this wailing multitude without shedding tears, he is marked out as a dangerous person, who cries with his mouth, but has no feeling of sympathy for the dead. He may be accused of having to do with the death; he may be accused even of causing it; he may be smelt out afterwards as a witch and killed. Mothers go out alone and wail for their babies in the veldt or moorland. For a slave captured who dies, they wail not, nor for those killed for witchcraft.

During the digging season, if death occurs in a village, they fast for a day, and give up work. They offer sacrifice in the form of a sheep or buck, which are cleansed by the priest who performs the ceremony, and then go back again to their town. The indunas or headmen of the villages have private little villages of their own, where they are buried, whether they die there or not. At an induna's death there is much wailing and weeping, and within a year of it a second great gathering for this purpose is convened. The friends and relatives from all parts of the country assemble at the kraal of which he had the oversight, and there for three days they drink beer, eat beef, and mourn for him. From the time of his death until then his spirit has been wandering about in the forest in a state of unrest, but during this second wailing, in their songs and requiems, they call back his spirit to the village to remain there for all time. So it comes about that the induna's spirit is supposed to hover over and around the place in which he lived before his death.

Certain snakes are looking round when people die, and the spirits of dead men are believed to go into them on leaving the body. In cases of sudden illness at headquarters certain ceremonies are performed forthwith. There are doctors whose special function it is to attend to this. Roots are dug up, ground into powder, mixed with water, or the blood of a goat or an ox, as the case may be, and put in a wooden dish. In this anointing oil the doctor dips the end of a giraffe's tail, and then sprinkles the sick person, his hut, yard, servants, garden, or the place where he was taken ill, in order to break the witchcraft by which some ill-disposed person has caused this sickness.

There are no burial scandals in the land, as there are no places set apart as graveyards. Most bodies are buried beneath thorn trees and bushes just outside the village, not in a lying but a sitting posture, with their faces turned towards the rising sun, and their hands and feet tied together. The indunas and other headmen are buried in their own huts.

A witch's relatives dare not wail publicly. Outwardly they appear to be glad, like the rest.

The Matabele have few thoughts as to the state after death. There are no idols to whom they can pray on behalf of their departed dead, unless you call their spears, shields, and clubs idols. These, it may be said, are more reverenced than many of the idols of India and China. But such a thing as

SICKNESS AND DEATH.

prayer to an idol of wood or stone is not known in the land.

After death the spirit enters an ox, a snake, a buffalo, or some other wild animal. Talking with the chief one day on this subject, he said that bad men had their abode in the spirit-world right away in the forest in a lonely wilderness, far removed from all people, while those whom they thought good were called back by their wailing and singing relatives at the time of death, to live in and around their former dwelling.

Their usual custom of offering sacrifice to the departed spirit is by slaughtering an ox or a sheep, near to the grave; the feet, ears, tail, nose, mouth, and the tip of its tongue are cut off, put into a pot and boiled together with a number of medicinal roots which are specially used for that purpose. When all is cooked sufficiently, then the near relatives call upon the departed one in this fashion : ' My father (or mother, as the case may be), why was it you died and left me ? I was not the cause of your death. You were always kind to me, and we loved each other so. My hands are clean : I did not bewitch you. My heart is white towards you, for here I am at your grave with food for you to eat : come and partake of it ; I cannot. Guard me from the evil spirits in your realm, come and preside over my hut at home, and be my helper ! ' This done, the mourner goes to the river to wash, and then to the priest, who purifies him from any evil taints he may have received in offering sacrifice to the dead ; after which he returns home again to his own people.

If a man is kicked or horned by an ox or a wild animal, it is the spirit of one of his relatives who had a grudge against him on earth, and now pays him back for some old score or other. In the royal circle a fixed number of pure black oxen are set apart, as retaining the spirits of their ancestors, and on this account they are never slaughtered; the number being replenished when any old ones die. When a sick man calls the doctor to ask what is the cause of his illness, he may be told that a certain old friend of his who died in the long ago has come to trouble him, and wants him to die; but the doctor adds: 'If you pay me a sheep, I will intercede on your behalf with some other spirits to induce this one to leave you alone, and then you will recover from your sickness.' Or the sick man may be sent for a certain medicine which some particular doctor has, and which has power over this wicked spirit to drive it away. He may be sent to the white man or the missionary. He believes all this; and more than one has come on this account to me for medicine. But in health no one ever troubles himself about those who have died. It is a rule never to talk about them, nor their condition; the present is everything. A hand-to-mouth existence, with plenty to eat and drink, is their *summum bonum*, and in this is included an occasional raid upon some neighbouring tribe for plunder in the form of women and children, cattle and buck and sheep.

MR. CARNEGIE'S WAGGON EN ROUTE FOR MATABELE LAND.

CHAPTER VIII.

CHRISTIAN WORK AMONG THE MATABELE.

THE Gospel has been preached among the Matabele people for many years; but as with Umzilikazi, so with Lobengula, the attitude of the chief has been unfavourable. The old king was an example to the whole tribe, and remained so until his death, living and dying a heathen. It was dangerous for any one to stay long with the missionaries, for this roused suspicion; and rather than be suspected of witchcraft, scores who heard them left and returned to their heathen ways of life. They might go and beg from the missionaries, ask for beads, knives, and medicines, but they were cold, indifferent, and unconcerned in all that related to Christian teaching. Ask them why this was, and they would tell you, 'The king does not do more. If it is not good for him to learn, it cannot be for us; we look to him for example in everything.' This was the position which the chief occupied from the very first, and it was a bar to progress.

Lobengula in his turn has listened to the most earnest pleadings, but both himself and his warriors scorn a gospel of peace. The people have often shown signs of attachment to the Christian teacher, and there have been occasional instances of deeper feeling; indirect results of Christian influence appear, but the trial of faith and patience has been long protracted, and now nothing seems possible but to await new opportunities, in dependence upon God and His grace.

As it is impossible to measure the extent of God's work in the churches at home, so also may this be said with truth in regard to that work in the foreign field abroad. To measure the work of God in Matabele land would be very difficult. It is impossible to do it, and for this reason: you cannot measure success in God's work anywhere by means of man's tape line. If success means so many numbers in tabulated forms, there is very little to record; but if it means an outward Christian example in the very midst of warlike heathenism, the Matabele Mission has not been a failure. There are a few even there who have not bowed the knee to Lobengula. Besides, to live for ten years in a savage country, and to be able to say, when you return home on furlough, that there is none like Christ in the world, means something in favour of Christianity, and the power of God in the heart of man. It has been laid upon me to give my life to this Mission, and that life can only endure hardness there, and be useful, just in so far as the prayers in the churches at home are practical, believing, and earnest.

But what about the history of the Mission in that land? It would only make the reader sad if I were to dwell too long upon the dark side of its history, to relate the thankless treatment borne in silence at the ruthless hands of the Matabele; standing often surrounded by warriors brandishing their clubs and spears above your head, and shaking their shields in your face, and having your beard pulled sometimes; all this, together with other experiences which need not be mentioned, of hopes deferred and blighted when you were expecting better days in your work, when in vain you pleaded with the king for his help and influence to assist you—I say to write such details as these might not be of so much interest as a long tabulated list of numbers, and these are not forthcoming so far as the Matabele Mission is concerned. Yet we make bold to say it is not a hopeless task endeavouring to teach these war-loving Matabele to do justly, love mercy, and walk humbly with God.

In 1860, when the first missionaries arrived in the country along with Dr. Moffat, the father of Lobengula—Umzilikazi—showed great reluctance in giving his consent to that Mission being established, by the act that for months he kept them waiting in suspense before giving them his decision that they might remain in the land. There was a formal meeting convened by the king and his indunas, to whom he addressed these words: 'Do you see these white men sitting over there?' They replied: 'Yes, great chief, we see them.' 'They have come to be your *abafundisi* "teachers," to teach you the "Book," or Word of God.' But how far these words were sincere you may judge from the results which followed them. Who was the god and idol of the Matabeles just then? Umzilikazi himself, to be sure. The homage, minds, and wills of the people were his; everything and everybody belonged to him, who was the monarch of all he surveyed, and his rights there was none to dispute. He was the example of the whole tribe, he preferred heathenism to Christianity, and lived and died and was buried with heathen ceremonies. Now and again some of the people would manifest real earnestness for the truth, and would continue for months in all sincerity in search of it. They would often say: 'Yes, these white men are right; their words are the words of God, who is good, and we believe it.' To declare openly you were a Christian then meant banishment or death, and this Matabele heathenism, horrible as it is, was to them better than that any day.

Lobengula was very much like his father, so far as the teaching and educating of his people are concerned. I did not know the old king, but have had ten years' experience in making myself acquainted with the present chief of the tribe. Often, and times without number, have I spoken and urged upon Lobengula to lend us his assistance in our mission work; and when pleading with him to ask some of the fathers in our neighbouring town to allow their children to come to us he replied: 'I am not the father of these children, and cannot say anything about it.' He tolerated us in the country, but did nothing more in return for the many kind words and actions which he received from us. He was the king, independent, great, mighty, and afraid of nobody or anything. He wanted to enjoy the blessings of civilisation without its laws. Having mentioned the fact of my furlough to Lobengula about a year previous to my return to this country, I asked him what kind of a report I should have to give, seeing he was so indifferent towards the progress of our work. He replied: 'You will tell them what you have seen.'

It was hoped at one time he would become a convert to Christianity. The Rev. W. Sykes told me how he used to sit and talk with him for hours together about his giving up ruling the tribe by heathen laws, in which live the awful fiends of witchcraft, injustice, and cruelty, and urged upon him to adopt the more merciful and excellent way of governing his people by the just and Christian principles of our Saviour Jesus Christ. To this he gave some attention, though he was not a very promising pupil, by wearing European clothing, having respect for the Sabbath, and allowing the missionaries to go anywhere, preaching the Gospel among the towns and villages.

It was the one fond dream of Mr. Sykes' life to try and win him over to Christianity. But the arrival of Hlegisana from Hope Town, in Cape Colony, put a stop to all this. This coloured man professed to have powerful medicines, by means of which he could sharpen the spears of Lobengula's warriors and make them successful in war. He caused the chief to believe that the missionary was a man of peace, did not encourage war in any shape or form, and if he accepted his principles he would never be a great king like unto his father, whose death was compared to the falling of a mountain; besides, this would mean a new departure, and a serious one too, the throwing over the old habits and heathen customs of the tribe. Thus it became apparent that the king must choose between the army doctor and the missionary. It was evident he could not be a Christian chief and a heathen at one and the same time, and he decided to listen to the army doctor, and the missionary from that time sat outside the king's hut, and the army doctor inside with the king.

There is no principle of progress or prosperity in heathenism or its laws either, and you need not be surprised to learn that the Matabele as a tribe are, practically speaking, in the same position, intellectually and morally, and in every other way, only a little more conceited, than they were thirty years ago. The great obstacle to progress of any kind is the chief, who won't allow his people to buy waggons, ploughs, spades, or agricultural implements of any kind, though guns, ammunition, and horses, with a view to foster the war spirit, are allowed. While he tolerated our being in the country, never, in any instance, was it known that he encouraged our work, or expressed himself pleased at what we did for himself and his people.

When this, then, is the attitude of the king towards the missionaries, what will that of the people be? We say to the king: 'Your witch-doctors deceive you, chief; listen not to their many words, for they contradict one another; they want your cattle and sheep. We speak but one word; we have one heart, we have one object in view, which is to teach your people to love God and one another.' The people are simply the slaves and dogs of the king, or, as they have told me more than once, the cattle which the herd-chief can drive in any direction and slaughter when he pleases. It matters not what you tell the king, he will just do as he likes, which is the conclusion of the whole thing. The people, then, fear, dread, shrink, and cringe before this great black king, whom they look upon as divine, who cannot err, who makes the rain, the new moon, sleeps with one eye open, who is god to them, whose power is unlimited, and against whom no one dare lift his little finger. If it is not good for the king to learn, neither is it for the people, who look to him for example in everything.

But apart from this dark element of heathenism against which we have been fighting, let it also be mentioned here in passing that our work has often been hindered by the immoral lives of white men who have been in the country. Yet, in spite of all this, there is a bright side to our work out yonder. There have been some noble examples of Christian heroism even in Matabele land. The foundation of the Church has been laid in the country, and the superstructure, though not high, has been commenced. Several converts have witnessed a noble confession to the power of saving grace. One faithful attender at the church at Inyati, when dying, was asked what he thought now about Jesus. The question was put to him: 'Where are you going now?' and the words came: 'I don't know, but Jesus does.' Another, who could read and write well, was accused of witchcraft, and before he knew it was tied up with his hands behind his back and marched away from the cattle post to his mock trial at Bulawayo, and from there was to be thrown to the wolves. On the way there, when asked what he would do now, he replied: 'Yes, in your eyes the witch-doctor has proved me guilty; but God knows I am not; you may kill my body, but my soul will go up there to live with Jesus.' To see with your own eyes a young man knocked down to the ground with a club because he refused to go back and live as a heathen in the native town; to see his hot blood on the ground and on his face; to see tears in his eyes, and his silent appeal to me for help, which I could not give—to experience this makes you feel that you have not lived for ten years in vain in Matabele land. For some of these natives to come and say good-bye, thank you for your work among them, and press you into a promise to return, means much to me. If God has not been manifesting His power there slowly and silently during the last ten years, then all I can say is, my deepest convictions are wrong, and my hope is vain. We have made progress; it has been slow, many-sided, but real, sure, and abiding. Behind these instances cited lies the true foundation on which the future Church of the country is to be built.

What, then, are the prospects of missionary work in Matabele land? The recent events in that country, in my judgment, point in one direction only. We expect great things on our return to our mission station at Hope Fountain. One great obstacle of fear and dread in the way of our past progress—the club of Lobengula—has been broken. The people now will not point any more to Bulawayo with their fingers as their final argument to silence their tongue from confessing Christ; they will no longer be in fear and dread of that heathen monarch's tyrannical power to crush their ambition, enterprise, and desire for knowledge; they will live in security, being able to hold what belongs to them ; to buy ploughs and waggons ; to trade, barter, buy, and sell ; to associate with the white man, to live near him, work for him, and enjoy the fruit of their toil. There will be no more slavery in the land, nor children brought to you for sale.

The woman, too, will have some room to live, and have some reason to rejoice that she is free from the thraldom of her heathen master. One man now will be as good as another, and Justice will raise her head, and witchcraft and bone-throwing will bow their heads and die. A new value will be put upon human life, and no one will be foully and innocently murdered by savage men. A new era will begin in the history of the country, and the people will be free. The current of their thoughts and feelings will be directed into another channel—that of progress, education, civilisation, and Christianity. Therefore, the future is full of hope and bright prospects. A chance is held out now such as never was before in their history, and many there be who will embrace it, rejoice in it, accept it, and through it become useful neighbours and honourable citizens in that fair and lovely country. The widow's wail and the orphan's cry will also cease, and instead we hope to see churches and schools planted all over the land.

Now is the grand opportunity of Christianising the Matabele. Instead of four there should be eight missionaries stationed in the country, and before other eight years will have passed Matabele land will have become one of the most inviting of missionary fields.

KHAMA.

CHAPTER IX.

KHAMA, THE BECHWANA CHRISTIAN CHIEF.

THE eyes of the civilised world are once more intently fixed upon South Africa, for the old struggle for mastery between antagonistic races has again reached an acute stage. Long foreseen, inevitable indeed from the first establishment of the Chartered Company, the latent hostility of the Matabele has broken forth, and the impis of Lobengula have tried their strength in open conflict with the white man's forces. Assegais and battle-axes on the one side are no match for Martini rifles and Maxim guns on the other. The Matabele power has apparently been broken on the first collision.

The Matabele, in spite of all the influences brought to bear upon them, are to-day what they were between sixty and seventy years ago, when, leaving Zululand, they carved out for themselves a new territory in the northern part of Bechwanaland. As then, so now, they are turbulent, sanguinary, untamed and apparently untamable horde of savages, the willing victims of gross superstition and abominable vices and practices. War and bloodshed are their delight. Lobengula, their chief, is not as black as he is painted. He is not altogether destitute of virtues—

witness his readiness to furnish escorts for foreigners who were leaving his country in anticipation of the coming fight; but for all that he stands forth as the embodiment of the very worst features of native African character.

In sharp contrast with the head of the Matabele there stands forth with equal prominence his hereditary foe, Khama, the vigorous chief of the Bamangwatos, whose career we propose briefly to trace. Whilst Lobengula has steadily refused to accept anything that savoured of Christianity or European civilisation, Khama has heartily welcomed both. Together with his headmen and the tribe he so ably and so wisely rules, he has sought to adapt himself to the new environment, and with one striking exception— the white man's strong drink, which he will not allow to be brought into his land—Khama readily accepts the products of civilisation that are offered him. The issue of this intelligent policy is that his country is under British protection. We must regret the necessity which summoned him and his men again into the field.

The Bamangwatos are of Bechwana origin, and they speak the Sechwana tongue. They, the Bakwenas, and the Bangwaketses spring from one common stock. Their traditions do not carry them back very far. They have preserved the names of seven successive chiefs, but beyond this their historical monuments do not reach. In the days of Khama's great-grandfather part of the tribe moved to the west and settled in the region of Lake Ngami, the rest remaining in the old quarters with Shoshong as the head town. Situated at the foot of a mountain range, with a stream issuing from the gorge as a water supply, this town of grass-roofed huts, containing a population of some 30,000 people, was for many years one of the most important places in Bechwana land. Latterly it has been deserted for a new settlement at Phalapye, which lies among the Cwapong mountains, about a hundred miles to the north-east of the old capital.

Khama,[1] whose early history is recorded at considerable length in the Rev. John Mackenzie's *Ten Years North of the Orange River,* to which this chapter is largely indebted, is the eldest son of the heathen chief Sekhome. He was still a young man when, in 1862, Messrs. Price and Mackenzie, missionaries of the London Missionary Society, arrived in Shoshong with the intention of commencing work. Three years before a German missionary belonging to the Hermannsburg Society had begun a mission there, but, owing to a misunderstanding with the home authorities, this good brother was left without supplies, and had to support himself by means of trading. Indeed, it was thought that he had withdrawn from the station, but this proved incorrect. For a time he continued to carry on a little work, but eventually retired in favour of the new-comers, his relations with whom had been from the first of a perfectly friendly nature. Khama soon evinced great interest in the Christian services and teaching which were started. Naturally of a frank and affectionate

---

[1] Sometimes written Khama, sometimes also Kgama.

I

disposition, he seemed to respond forthwith to the higher influence now brought to bear upon him. He became the fast friend of the missionaries, a regular attendant at school and worship, and soon learned to distrust the ancestral charms and superstitions.

Two significant incidents during a Matabele raid which occurred in 1862 will serve to illustrate his character. Alarmed at the approach of their warlike neighbours, the Bamangwato women betook themselves to the mountains for hiding, whilst their husbands, brothers, and sons prepared for the conflict. Mrs. Mackenzie was consequently left in Shoshong as the sole representative of her sex. A night of fearful suspense passed, but the dreaded Matabele did not come. The next day Khama came to the rescue with the suggestion, 'Let Ma-Willie' (the mother of Willie, as Mrs. Mackenzie was called by them) 'go to the mountain beside my mother, and the Matabele will then reach her only when we are all dead;' meaning that they would defend her just as they were determined to defend their own mothers.

The second incident was when the Bamangwatos were on the point of going forth to oppose the Matabele warriors. Sekhome, as head of the tribe, was also *ngaka,* or sorcerer, and in this capacity was busily occupied in studying his divination bones and repeating his incantations. Khama, with the impetuous ardour of a young man eager for the fray, and, under the influence of Scripture teaching, already sceptical as to the power and worth of sorcery and charms, abruptly interrupted his father by saying that he was spending far too much time

KHAMA, BECHWANA CHRISTIAN CHIEF. 115

over these things, and that as for himself he wished to fight without delay, and have done with it.

The raid referred to was the first that for several years the Matabele had ventured on. Formerly their impis passed through the Bamangwato country year after year, lifting cattle, destroying gardens, and driving the people to the mountains, but at length the Bamangwatos made a stand. In a stirring speech a young brave roused his countrymen to resistance. They attacked the Matabele, recovered their stolen cattle, and inflicted severe punishment upon the invaders. Subsequently when Moselekaste, the Matabele king, sent messengers demanding tribute, Sekhome boldly but brutally killed these envoys, as a plain indication of his refusal to acknowledge allegiance to the Zulu intruder. This determined attitude was not without effect. Weaker tribes round about were drawn to the Bamangwatos, whilst the Matabele learned that they had met with a foe equal to themselves in prowess and power.

Khama's remonstrance gave him that first taste of war for which he so eagerly longed. His father took it in good part, and at once ordered the two youngest regiments of his army, those of which his two sons, Khama and Khamana, were the heads, to advance and attack the enemy. These young bloods, some two hundred in number, most of whom carried firearms, and eight of whom were on horseback, set forth at once, and late in the afternoon came in sight of the Matabele, who were marching in three companies, two of them together. Charging these two, the Bamangwatos fairly routed them, the superiority of gun over spear giving them the victory. In the meantime, however, the third company of Matabele, who were at a distance, hearing the report of guns, stealthily approached the Bamangwatos from the rear. This demoralised them and compelled them to retreat, leaving about a score of their number dead on the field. Khama's behaviour from first to last was marked by great courage and resource, and from that day downwards the Matabele have left the Bamangwatos alone.

Not content with the amount of success he had achieved, Sekhome organised a raid of his own. Keeping his project a secret from Khama, he despatched a cattle-lifting expedition, with instructions to bring back from the Matabele cattle-posts as many oxen as possible, these being, as he alleged, his own property that had been lawlessly stolen. The raid was successful, and large herds of oxen, sheep, and goats were secured and brought back. The sequel furnishes a further illustration of Khama's character. His father offered him what must have been a most tempting present in the shape of a liberal proportion of the booty, but he refused to accept it. He entirely disapproved of the expedition, and would not compromise himself by sharing its spoils.

The difference between father and son was not limited to these matters, but was deep-seated, and grew at length to most serious proportions. Sekhome, rain-maker and sorcerer, took frequent opportunities of visiting Mr. Mackenzie and Mr. Price. He would talk freely about religion, but invariably ended by saying that the Word of God was 'far' from him, that his heart was 'crooked' and would not follow its teaching. He lacked the moral earnestness and courage to do what he confessed freely that he ought to do. Consequently he remained a heathen to the last. Khama, on the other hand, whilst retaining the love of power and autocratic temper natural to the son of a ruler, yielded himself more and more fully to the guidance of the Bible. Even Sekhome, who was jealous and more than half afraid of his powerful son, had to acknowledge that Khama's heart was not crooked like his own, not prone to falsehood and deceit as he was, but 'right.' 'Yes,' he said, on one occasion, 'Khama's heart is right.' To know the truth is one thing; to obey it is another. Sekhome would not, could not, with his 'crooked' ways (which he had no wish to change), follow a right course himself, nor was he willing to allow Khama and Khamana to follow this either. He therefore set himself the task of bending their wills until they should yield to the same devious practices as satisfied his own dark heart.

The story of this African chief's defeat in his prolonged attempt to coerce his sons' conscience is intensely interesting and pathetic. It began in 1865, when the ceremony of *boguera*, or circumcision, was celebrated with the usual obscene rites. To his great surprise and indignation, Sekhome found his sons unwilling to attend the ceremony. He was deeply offended, and threatened them with severe penalties for their disobedience. By dint of promises and threats he succeeded in winning over two of his sons, but Khama and two others resolutely refused to yield. That was a time of much trial for the mission. Attendance at school or worship was regarded as treason against the chief, and those who courageously came notwithstanding were marked men, and had to endure persecution, privation, and contumely. Poor Khama and Khamana were practically disowned.

Nothing daunted, however, the two young chiefs held nobly on their way. Further trouble arose in reference to their marriage relations. They had married sisters, and, as Christians, refused to 'add to' the number of their wives. Yet by this refusal they gave great offence not only to their father, but also to the headmen of the town, whose daughters by marriage with the king's sons would have received elevation in rank and importance. Sekhome, happening to remember that some years before he had negotiated a marriage between Khama and the daughter of one of his headmen who was a sorcerer, determined to force Khama to take this girl as his proper wife, and to degrade Mabese, his actual wife, to an inferior position. Khama's answer was a respectful and straightforward one. 'I refuse,' he said, 'on account of the Word of God, to take a second wife; but you know that I was always averse to this woman, having declined to receive her from you as my wife before I became a Christian.... Lay the hardest task upon me with reference to hunting elephants for ivory, or any service you can think of as a token of my obedience, but I cannot take the daughter of Pelutona to wife.' Sekhome, however, overreached himself. His fury on the one side and the dignified forbearance of his sons on the other, produced a very different effect from what he intended. The people lost their feeling of loyalty to him, and more and more favoured Khama and his brother. At last he discovered his weakness. Ordering his headmen to fire upon the huts in which his sons were, he found none willing to obey his command. Realising the position, he became alarmed for his own safety, and fled in terror to a place of hiding, fully expecting that his sons would retaliate. But the two young chiefs had no such thought, and at once sent a messenger to reassure him. They would not lift a hand against him.

But the wretched father would not desist from his vile schemes. He plotted to prevent his son's accession to power; even went the length of hiring a Matabele soldier to murder Khama, and, inflamed by jealousy at the evident superiority of his sons to himself, could not rest day nor night. Europeans did not hesitate to let him see what they thought of his conduct, and one day, when he was indulging in fierce denunciation of his refractory children, a missionary promptly checked him with the bold statement that 'there was not another chief in Bechwana land that had such obedient sons.' Eventually matters became so critical that Khama determined to retire to a stronghold in the mountains, so as to keep out of his father's way. Charms failing to dislodge him, Sekhome besieged Khama in that mountain stronghold, and after eight days a peace was patched up, on the understanding that Khama returned to the town. The next move on the part of Sekhome was to invite his brother Macheng to return to Shoshong.

After he had been there for several weeks he introduced him to the people as their king, and then weakly sought relief from his troubles, mostly of his own making, by ignominious flight. Writing of this period, Dr. von Gustav Fritsch, an educated German gentleman and man of scientific reputation, who in 1865 paid a visit to Shoshong, says: 'I am glad by my acquaintanceship with Khama to have had an opportunity of mentioning a black whom I would under no circumstances be ashamed to call my friend. The simple, modest, and at the same time noble, deportment of this chief's son awoke a delightful feeling which till then I had never experienced in the company of black men.'

Sekhome's flight took place in 1866, and for six years Macheng ruled in his stead. This prince had been chief in bygone days, and was considered by many to be the rightful head of the tribe, but had been forced into exile by his brother Sekhome, who, however, for his own satisfaction, had now recalled him. For a time there was peace, but Macheng soon began to show signs of unfitness for the post he filled. The unchanged heathenism of his heart manifested itself both in the animalism of his life and in his jealousy of the influence of Christianity. His chief delights were gluttony and drunkenness; and absorbed in a continual round of eating, drinking, and sleeping, he neglected the duties of chieftainship, and permitted anarchy and misrule to have full sway. Then, seeing that a growing number of his people were coming under the influence of Christian teaching, he became suspicious of the missionaries. At length he publicly complained one day in the *khotla* or enclosure, that 'there was now another chief in the town—the Word of God! and that Macheng was not first but second.' Khama and his brother he was specially jealous of, and his dislike to them grew stronger and more pronounced.

Thus it came about that Khama's life-story was again a troubled one. The schemes of a father were succeeded by those of an uncle, both intent on his ruin. His own and his brother Khamana's popularity was greater than ever, but this only made matters so much the worse. To show his resentment, Macheng even went the length of despatching an expedition, of which Khama and his regiment formed part, with an inferior officer placed at the head of it. But the Bamangwatos ignored the appointment, refused to have any leader but Khama, and at once installed him in command. This gave mortal offence to the king. Space will not allow us to describe in detail the plots and counterplots that occupied the next few years. In self-defence, and to prevent the break-up of the tribe, the two young chiefs had at last to assert themselves, and, having first urged their father to return, which he refused to do, they, with the aid of Sechele, chief of the Bakwenas, got rid of Macheng by driving him into exile. This was in September, 1872. Khama was elected chief, a position which he accepted, but with characteristic prudence. He said to the assembled people: 'I have not fought for the chieftainship, but for my life. As to my father, I sent Khamana to invite him and to bring him home. He refused my invitation, and thus increased the danger in which my life was placed. I shall not ask him again; it is for you, Bamangwatos, to send for him, and to bring him back again.' He thus threw the responsibility upon the headmen.

One of Khama's first acts as king was to define his attitude towards heathenism on the one hand and Christianity on the other. Amongst other time-honoured ceremonies was one connected with seed-time and harvest. Not until sundry charms, incantations, and spells had been duly employed by the chief could the gardens and fields be sown in spring or reaped in autumn. So with many other things. After consultation with the missionaries—the Rev. John Mackenzie and the Rev. D. Hepburn, who had succeeded Mr. Price—Khama assembled his people in his *khotla* and emphatically announced his own adherence to the Word of God. 'He would not prohibit heathen ceremonies, but they must not be performed in his *khotla*, and as their chief he would contribute nothing towards them. He was about, by public prayer to Almighty God, to ask a blessing upon their seed-sowing, and afterwards would set to work. Whoever wished to have his seed charmed could do so at his own expense, but he himself had no such custom now, any more than in former years.' This speech, the language and tone of which were so unmistakable, was well received by the people, and Mr. Mackenzie tells us that he felt at its close that Khama was, both in his own and in the tribe's estimation, further removed from heathenism than he was before he had thus decisively declared his policy.

For twent -one years Khama has been in power,

and his reign throughout had been in thorough harmony with that early declaration. All who know him bear testimony to his consistent life, his sagacious and enlightened rule, and to the general strength, probity, and nobility of his character. At the beginning of his reign he made one serious mistake, which involved him in much difficulty and trial. In the face of his declaration that he would not again recall his father, Sekhome, he did at the end of 1872 invite the old man back. What his motives were in doing so it is difficult to understand, but it proved to be a disastrous move. Sekhome returned, and, cunning heathen as he was, at once set to work trying to regain his former ascendency over the tribe. He revived former rites and practices, and by carefully fostering the ambition of Khamana and manifesting great regard for him, whilst ignoring Khama, he succeeded in sowing the seeds of mutual distrust and in setting the brothers against one another. Recognising his mistake, Khama endeavoured to rectify it, but it was not until he had first of all withdrawn to a distance, and had been joined by the people, who eagerly flocked to his standard, that he felt able to cope with his treacherous father and now hostile brother. In February, 1875, he led his followers to battle. A fight for the possession of Shoshong followed, and in this Khama was victorious. Sekhome and Khamana took to flight, and henceforth Khama's authority was firmly established.

Parricidal and fratricidal contests appear to belong to the normal conditions of African tribal life, and in the struggles we have briefly recorded there was little of exceptional character, apart from the new element introduced by Christianity, which involved a fresh line of cleavage. But the retrospect was a sad one to the missionaries. Making all allowances for the ignorance and backward condition of the Bamangwatos, who had so recently and so partially emerged from barbarism, they greatly deplored the outbreak of war and commotion. Especially were they distressed at the disagreement between the two brothers. Looking back upon that eventful period, Mr. Mackenzie records: 'When the first indications of alienation made their appearance I called them again and again into my study, reasoned and prayed with them, and besought them to understand one another, and to love as brethren. The result was only temporary: the one was ambitious; suspicion filled the mind of the other.' One regrets that any stain should rest upon the fair fame of Khama, but in the earlier stages of his quarrel with his brother he was hardly true to the nobler side of his character. The subsequent developments of the quarrel, however, clearly showed that Khamana was chiefly to blame.

Undoubtedly this chief stands out conspicuously among South African princes as the finest, noblest of them all. He rules with a firm hand, is soldierly in bearing, a keen sportsman, a good rider, every inch a man; but combined with this strength there is remarkable patience, gentleness, and kindliness of disposition, and none who know him doubt his sincerity or earnestness as a Christian. The remarkable way in which by the force of his own example and conduct he has led his people forward in the pathway of enlightened Christian progress furnishes striking evidence of this. Witchcraft and 'smelling out' are illegal, and if practised at all must be practised in secret. Four or five years ago he accomplished the feat of removing his town from Shoshong to Phalapye, as previously stated, the water supply at the former place no longer meeting the requirements of the tribe; and in his new town he has secured comforts and advantages possessed by few, if any, South African peoples.

More wonderful even than the moral and social elevation of the Bamangwatos is that of some of the wretched Bakalaharis and other subject tribes, who under Khama's benign and sagacious sovereignty have been uplifted from the lowest depths of human degradation. Mr. Selous, the famous hunter, has been deeply impressed with this. In an address delivered to the South African Philosophical Society, Mr. Selous said :—

'A generation ago all the Bakalahari lived the life described by Dr. Livingstone and others. They wandered continually, under a burning sun, over the heated sands of the Kalahari, without any fixed habitation, and ever and always engaged in a terrible struggle for existence, living on berries and bulbs and roots, on snakes and toads and lizards, with an occasional glorious feast on a fat eland, giraffe, or zebra, caught in a pitfall; sucking up water through reeds, and spitting it into the ostrich egg-shells, in which they were wont to carry it, and altogether leading a life of bitter grinding hardship from the cradle to the grave. In fact, they were utter savages;

joyless, soulless animals, believing nothing, hoping nothing, but, unlike Sir Walter Scott's Bothwell, fearing much, for they were sore oppressed by their Bechwana masters, and often became the prey of the lions and hyenas that roamed the deserts as well as they. Now many of the wild people have been induced by Khama to give up their nomadic life. He supplied them with seed corn, and, as may be seen at Klabala and other places, the Bakalaharis of the present day hoe up large expanses of ground, and grow so much corn that, except in seasons of drought, they know not the famine from which their forefathers were continually suffering. In addition to this, Khama and his headmen have given them cattle, sheep and goats, to tend for them, from which they obtain a constant supply of milk. In fact, it may be said that Khama has successfully commenced the work of converting a tribe of miserable nomadic savages into a happy pastoral people.'

We may add, what Mr. Selous omits, that Khama's philanthropy is the direct fruit of Khama's Christianity, and is a touching and beautiful illustration of practical godliness and of faith in the power of kindness and love. Mr. Selous's estimate of the chief's character, however, is high. He says:—

'I should like to add a few words to the very general tribute of praise that has been accorded him. To myself personally he has always been most kind and courteous, and I believe him to be a strictly upright and honourable man. I might say much more, but I have said enough to show that I have a high appreciation of his character. Many of his

KHAMA, BECHWANA CHRISTIAN CHIEF.

headmen, too—amongst whom I may mention some special friends of mine, such as Kwati, Tinkin, Makamani, and Musiakabo—I have always found to be thoroughly trustworthy, reliable men, ready to do a friend a service without expecting payment for it— a trait of character I have never yet met with in a wild, uncivilised Kafir, whose motto always appears to be to give or do nothing for nothing, and as little as possible for sixpence.'

Khama's relations to the outside world have been mutually advantageous. His drastic temperance measures and resolute refusal to admit strong drink have thus far been respected, and dark would be the day in the country's history that saw the enforced introduction of 'Cape smoke.' The mission of Sir Charles Warren led to the British Protectorate, which Khama voluntarily accepted, and even sought. Hence the aid which the Bamangwato gave to the Chartered Company's forces.

Khama has no doubt himself as to the power that has made him what he is. He unhesitatingly ascribes it to the influence of Christ's Gospel, brought to him by the agents of the London Missionary Society, in whose hands the work has been entirely since 1862. The majority of the Bamangwatos are still very ignorant—must, indeed, be regarded as heathen; but the mission is making good progress. A handsome chapel, the finest in Bechwanaland, which cost the people £3000, was set apart for worship last year. The Rev. W. C. Willoughby is in charge of the station. In addition two ladies have been specially appointed for educational work among the women and girls. This appointment has given much satisfaction to Khama himself, who anticipates from it lasting blessing for his people.

Here we must leave him. If his future resemble his past, the name of this Bechwana chief will long be remembered with respect and admiration by all friends of South Africa, irrespective of colour, race, or creed. His virtues command the sympathy and esteem of a very wide circle. May he long be spared to manifest them! and may his son, Sekhome, prove a worthy son of his worthy sire! are the two best wishes we can have for the future prosperity of the Bamangwatos.

THE END.

LONDON: PRINTED BY WILLIAM CLOWES AND SONS, LIMITED, STAMFORD STREET AND CHARING CROSS.